The Romance of Lace

THE
ROMANCE
OF LACE

MARY EIRWEN JONES

SPRING BOOKS
LONDON

Published by

SPRING BOOKS

SPRING HOUSE · SPRING PLACE · LONDON N W 5

Printed in Czechoslovakia

CONTENTS

Introduction, page 9

Lace: Its Evolution, page 13

The Laces of Italy, page 37

The Laces of the Low Countries, page 61

The Laces of France, page 81

The Laces of Other European Countries, page 117

The Laces of Britain, page 137

Conclusion, page 171

Bibliography, page 172

1*

ILLUSTRATIONS

The Laughing Cavalier
    FRANZ HALS   Frontispiece
Needlepoint lace in the making   page 17
Lace Pillow with Bobbins   19
English. Flounce of machine-made lace. Twentieth century   19
English. Crochet lace. Nineteenth century   21
Egypto-Roman netting in linen and woollen threads   23
Venice. Collar of needlepoint lace. Seventeenth century   41
Italy. Three borders of reticella lace. Late sixteenth century   43
Italy. Flounce of needlepoint lace. Late seventeenth century   45
Venice. Lappets in needlepoint lace. Early eighteenth century   47
North Italy. Bobbin lace. Cuffs. Late seventeenth century   53
Italy. Milan. Bobbin lace panel à brides. Seventeenth century   55
Brussels. Shawl of pillow-made lace. Early nineteenth century   57
French. Probably Binche. Bobbin lace. Cap crown and lappets. Early nineteenth century   59
Mechlin. Bobbin lace. Part of a flounce. Early eighteenth century   73
Brussels. Pillow-made lace. Portion of an apron. Early eighteenth century   73
Flanders. Antwerp. Bobbin lace. Eighteenth century   75
Brussels. Point de Gaze. Fan mount. Needlepoint lace. Mid-nineteenth century   77
Brussels. Christening veil. Early nineteenth century   77

Brussels. Wedding veil. Early nineteenth century   page 79
France. Chantilly fan. Circa 1850–70   97
France. Needlepoint lace. Point de France. Late seventeenth century   99
France. Point d'Argentan. Flounce. Circa 1700   101
France. Lille. Veil. Mid-nineteenth century   103
France. Valenciennes. Bobbin lace. Four lappets or barbes. Early eighteenth century   109
France. Probably from Caen. Veil. Bobbin-made silk blonde. Mid-nineteenth century   111
Cyprus lace. Needlepoint. Nineteenth century   113
Czechoslovakian lace. Bobbin-made mat. Nineteenth century   113
Maltese lace. Flounce of pillow-made lace in cream-coloured silk. Early nineteenth century   115
Greek lace. Zante. Edging. Needlepoint. 1630   115
Portrait of a Lady Unknown. HANS HOLBEIN   129
England. Sampler of needlepoint lace. Early seventeenth century   131
Queen Elizabeth   133
English lace. Buckinghamshire. Shawl of Bobbin lace. Early nineteenth century   135
Great Britain. Needlelace. Mid-nineteenth century   157
Ireland. Irish point. Late nineteenth century   167
Ireland. Irish point. Collar. Mid-nineteenth century   168

Author's Note

'Art', declares John Galsworthy in the *Inn of Tranquillity*, 'is the great and universal refreshment.'

It is with faith in that dictum that this book has been compiled to serve in the nature of an *hors-d'œuvre* to the feast that awaits all those who care to pursue the enchanting study of lace-craft in all its many facets.

The author wishes to express heartfelt gratitude to H. M. the Queen for the use of illustrative matter and also to the authorities of the National Gallery and the Wallace Collection. She has received invaluable help and encouragement from the Victoria and Albert Museum, South Kensington, and the Needlework Development Scheme, Glasgow. She has received kindly assistance from the Librarians at Windsor Castle, the Keeper of the Folk Museum of Wales, St Fagans, Cardiff, and the Sisters of the Order of the Poor Clares, Kenmare, County Kerry, and from others who have contributed with information and illustrations.

Her sincere thanks are tendered to Mr William Rees, M.A., for various suggestions and criticisms and for the reading of the proofs.

INTRODUCTION

THE CHARM OF LACE has been acknowledged throughout the ages. A knowledge of the art and the romance attached to its historical evolution serves to emphasize and accentuate the worth of this delightful fabric. Museums and art galleries are rich in the possession of magnificent pieces of lace and many fine specimens have been preserved by private collectors.

Many of the laces represent the work of abbesses and nuns for lace was used extensively as a trimming for ecclesiastical garments and furnishings. Lace has, however, a broader significance for the layman. The greater proportion of old lace in existence today is a legacy from the fifteenth, sixteenth and seventeenth centuries. It is representative of times when lace was an important and an elegant accessory of dress.

In the Middle Ages, lace-workers achieved a high standard of excellence in their art. Continental lace-workers were the most expert. Inspired and trained by these, however, the lace-workers of Britain also created beautiful lace.

The lace fabrics of several countries enjoyed a vogue in turn. Sometimes the standard of achievement was raised as a result of rivalry. Demand invariably exceeded supply; large sums of money poured into that country where the lace created took precedence in fashion.

Sumptuary Laws

So extravagant a fashion did lace become at times that several monarchs passed at intervals sumptuary laws to control its use. Fundamentally, these sumptuary laws were intended to maintain class distinctions, to repress luxury and to discourage extravagance especially among what were termed the lower classes. These sumptuary laws were regulations controlling ostentatious expenditure on dress, ornament, furniture and food. From the early sixteenth century onward, the sumptuary laws which were passed in Britain may be said to have had an additional motive. They were occasioned largely by a desire to promote home industries.

The possession of fine lace was coveted, much of it being preserved in the nature of family heirlooms. Old laces were prominent items in wills. In 1728, Samuel Johnson wrote a letter to Boswell stating:

'Greek, sir, is like lace; every man gets as much of it as he can.'

Lace Honoured in Other Arts

Artists and poets realized the charm of lace and honoured it. Holbein in his *Portrait of a Lady* recorded an early development of 'lacis' on the linen head-dress she favoured. The

Venetian, the Flemish and the Dutch painters spent hours in representing the beauty of the fabric and were eminently successful in depicting it. Van Dyke's portraits testify to the generous use of lace on the elaborate costumes worn in the Stuart Period. Later, skilled artists such as Le Brun, Bailly and Berain, directed by court patronage, created beautiful patterns to be worked on net grounds.

Writers – poets in especial – praised the grace and beauty of lace. The lyric poet, Robert Herrick, writing in the second quarter of the seventeenth century, paid tribute to the charm of a wayward lace when he catalogued the details of 'A sweet disorder in the dress':

> An erring lace which here and there
> Enthrals the crimson stomacher.

Changes in Fashion

Towards the middle of the eighteenth century, the extravagances of linen and velvet and lace gave way to a simplicity – a simplicity which savoured of artificiality as sponsored by the royal court of France and copied with unreasoned slavishness by the other countries of Europe.

This pseudo-simplicity was not without its virtues. Clothing began to assume a more hygienic character. Robert Burns wrote his poem *To a Louse* at the close of the eighteenth century.

> Ha! whare ye gaun ye crowlin ferlie!
> Your impudence protects you sairly
> I canna say but ye strunt rarely
> Owre gauze and lace;
> Though faith I fear ye dine but sparely
> On sic a place.

The wearing of lace fell into decadence from the time of the French Revolution. That political and social tumult affected all classes of society. Relative values were changed drastically. The aristocracy sold their treasuries of lace. The lace industries of many countries were affected adversely. The dress of men and women became simpler and lace came to be regarded as an ornamentation for women's costume only.

Machine-made Lace Flooded the Markets

A super-abundance of machine-made lace in the nineteenth and early twentieth centuries led to its becoming an ubiquitous fabric. Nevertheless, hand-made varieties were still treasured. The hand-made lace industries of the Continent were given a fillip from time to time by royal patronage. In Britain too, hand-workers were given encouragement. Queen Adelaide and Queen Victoria took special delight in the laces made in Britain – a delight which has become hereditary in the Royal house.

Collectors of Lace

The twentieth century has witnessed a discriminating interest in the laces of the past. In the auction rooms, connoisseurs congregate to compete for the possession of choice pieces. Beautiful specimens in public collections have their devotees. Everywhere there are lovers of the 'fairy fabric'. It may be that as they gaze at the exquisite designs and the gossamer thread, they crystallize within themselves something of the spirit of that charming poem by Mrs Thomas Ellis Baker,

> Let me grow lovely, growing old:
> So many fine things do;
> Laces and ivory and gold
> And silks need not be new.

LACE: ITS EVOLUTION

*Lace is an open-work fabric formed by interlacing, braiding
or twisting threads of flax, cotton, silk or metallic fibre.*

Terms used in Lace-craft

THE WORD LACE is derived from the Latin *lacinia*, the fringe or the hem of a garment. In the statutes of the Plantagenet period the term 'lacez', meaning an open-work fabric, is confused with 'laces', meaning the braids used for fastening sections of a garment.

Passement, a word spelt in many ways, was a general term for braids, gimps, laces made in a variety of threads. *Passement dentelle* came to be used for a lace with a toothed edge; this was abbreviated to *dentelle*.

Lace consisted of the ground, the '*entoilage*' and the '*toile*', or pattern, which at first was so firmly made that it resembled closely-knit linen.

The ground was made in needlepoint or '*au fuseau*', on the pillow. The ground was termed *à réseau, fond, champ, treille*. These had specialized names such as *fond clair, fond double*, Brussels ground, wire ground, trolly ground.

Brides, or bridges, united different parts of the fabric. These were usually very fine and showed exacting workmanship often being composed of one strand of thread button-holed over and bearing tiny picots or minute stars. The open-work stitches used as fillings were called *modes* or *jours*.

A raised cord, or *cordonnet*, introduced high relief into needlepoint laces. This was worked over with overcasting stitches or covered separately and then sewn in place. Venetian workers enhanced the *cordonnet* with *couronnes*, raised ornamentations super-imposed to as many as four times.

The outer edge of a lace was also called a *couronne*. The term *engrêlure* was given to a narrow edging which served to secure the stitches of the ground and which served as a border for sewing the lace on to a garment.

Lace-makers were often paid in lace-tokens. These were accepted as legitimate currency in the eighteenth century. Lace fabric was measured in ells. The English ell was fixed in 1101 and measured 45 inches. The Scotch ell was 37·2 inches. A French ell was 54 inches and a Flemish ell 27 inches.

Guipure lace involved the use of twisted silk and cartisane. The latter was a narrow strip of vellum or parchment covered with silk or metallic thread and used to form a stiff, raised pattern. This lace was made with the needle or with bobbins; the less cartisane used the better the lace, for it was not washable. Later *guipure* was used for pillow laces bearing a tape-like design.

Gueuse was a lace made of thick thread. It was known as *beggar's lace* and was used extensively by the poorer classes in France. The pattern consisted of flowers and was worked loosely in thick thread.

Mignonette was a fine pillow lace made in the neighbourhood of Paris, Normandy, Auvergne and Lorraine from Lille thread. It had a clear ground and was about two or three inches wide.

Campane was another narrow pillow lace. When made of white thread it was used to trim – and sometimes to repair – wider laces. It was also made in gold, silver and coloured threads.

Early Varieties

EARLY FRINGE WORK Ancient civilizations have bequeathed materials in the form of garments, furnishings and rugs ornamented with elaborate fringes. Worn edges and the unravelling of threads probably suggested a fringe. This was enhanced by the addition of ornamental stitches and the more elaborate combinations of these stitches formed the beginnings of lace.

As increased skill was attained, geometrical precision and design were introduced into the knotting of the fringe. Many garments taken from the ancient tombs of Assyria and Egypt were decorated in this way.

The netting of threads was known at an early epoch. Ancient manuscripts make frequent reference to it but some confusion is wrought by the failure of the Chaldaic, Hebrew and Arabic writers to distinguish clearly between network and early lace.

EARLY NETWORK Elaborate forms of early network have been found in the tombs of Ancient Egypt. The weavers of this fabric are described in *Isaiah* XI. 9. 'They that work in fine flax and they that weave networks.' Network was used as a covering for the head and the breast. It may have had some religious significance, for, fastened to many of the specimens taken from the ancient tombs, were miniature deities of remarkable workmanship fashioned in metal or porcelain.

VARIETIES OF NETTING It is known that the oldest processes of Coptic netting involved the use of a four-sided frame. A double warp was stretched across and a special rod was used to keep the threads apart. The weaver knotted or plaited the threads with his fingers and commenced the work from the centre of the frame.

By another process, the warp and weft threads were twisted at the places where they intersected. The weft was called the *buratto*, a name which has been preserved in the Italian name for this kind of netting. This simple form of network was almost universally known among early civilizations. It was much in use among the early Egyptians. The Swiss lake-dwellers practised the craft. The Incas of Peru in the nineteenth century created fabrics made from cotton and vicuna wool, beautiful in texture and in colouring. These they adorned with what have proved to be some of the finest specimens of knotted netting with geometrical designs.

Another early variation, also created on a frame, was that in which warp and weft were knotted at each intersection in such a way that a design was built up from the actual knotting. The pattern was elementary but it served as a foundation for the type of lace which was known in later ages as *réseau* or *filet brodé*.

A more ambitious form of early network and possibly representative of a more advanced stage of civilization, was that of netting over a circular disc. The pattern was adapted to the shape and size of the disc. Later lace-workers retained this process as a basis for their work. It is shown in the *toile d'araignée of* France, in the sun pattern of the *punto de Cataluna* and the *nanduti* of South America.

PREHISTORIC LACE SPECIMEN Homer makes reference to net veils made from woven gold, and it is recorded that the Emperor Nero wore a net covering of gold threads. Gold lace in a simple form was in established use. When an early Scandinavian barrow was opened at Wareham in Dorsetshire, a small piece of gold lace was discovered. It was worked in a lozenge pattern. Gold thread netting was used to trim the garments of the nobles and ecclesiasts in Anglo-Saxon times and its use was continued in the Middle Ages. The finest qualities of this early gold lace were obtained from Cyprus. Later there was an increased demand for the 'fringe of gold of Venys', the gold and silver threads of which were obtained from Genoa and Lucca.

Medieval Varieties

DARNED NETTING Lace in the Middle Ages had a wide connotation. An early form was that known as darned netting. It was sometimes called darned lace or spider work. It was also known as *Ouvrages Masches*, *Opus Araneum* and *Lacis*. This form of lace-work had many devotees in Italy, particularly in Siena. The work was, as a consequence, sometimes referred to as *Siena Point*. The plain net of square meshes was called *réseau*, *rezel* or *rezeuil* and was used for bed-curtains and vallances. On this ground a pattern was darned. Sometimes the effect was colourful and brilliant for coloured silks were intermingled with gold and silver thread. The work resembled tapestry both in the counting of stitches and in the finished work.

RETICELLAS Reticellas or Greek point lace took precedence among other types of laces in the period 1480 to 1620. This variety of cut-work enjoyed a great vogue for it was used extensively on ecclesiastical garments, church cloths, shrouds and lay garments. It was familiar to many as a motif appearing on samplers. The pattern books relating to early needlework were expensive and difficult to obtain, and teachers taught the various patterns by means of 'sam-cloths' or samplers. Young folk showed their competency in the arts of needlework on these, causing the samplers to become treasured objects in themselves.

In reticella work geometrical patterns were popular, particularly in the earliest specimens. The work was done by means of buttonhole stitching. Picots or pearls were introduced at intervals. As time went on designs became more ornate but the stiff lines of geometrical patterns were still adhered to for the worker took heed of the right angles in the linen fabric caused by the intersection of threads. But even in the Middle Ages the needleworker negotiated circles, triangles and stars and created elaborate bars to link the units of the pattern.

CUT-WORK When linen was closely woven, the fabric was cut. Buttonhole stitching secured the edges and the spaces were filled or partly filled with decorative stitches. At first these spaces were small but as the workers grew more expert more and more of the foundation cloth was cut away. The stitchery used to block in the spaces grew more and more elaborate and ornamental. A high standard of work was achieved when the foundation was reduced to a few linen threads only. These were buttonholed over and the lines so formed were incorporated into the design.

THE QUINTAIN Yet more elaborate work was introduced into later forms of cut-work. Certain types were made on a light wooden frame. Threads were attached to the sides of this frame and these were crossed and interlaced according to a preconceived plan. A panel of fine cloth was attached beneath the threads. A usual name for this cloth was 'Quintain', a name derived from the town in Brittany where lawn of the best quality was manufactured. By means of firm buttonhole stitching, the network of threads was attached to the foundation of fine cloth. The stitching followed the lines of the pattern and the remainder of the lawn was cut away. The design itself remained on the foundation cloth and the buttonhole stitching served to introduce high relief. As the workers gained in experience and inspiration, methods and stitches of a more complex nature were introduced. By the early years of the sixteenth century many workers had dispensed with the foundation cloth. A pattern was drawn and worked on a parchment which was removed when the design was complete. The worker paid obeisance no longer to the right-angles of the warp and weft of a closely-woven linen.

DRAWN WORK Another form of early needlework which may be regarded as a forerunner of lace was drawn work. This was done on loosely-woven linen. This work was known by a variety of names – *Opus Tiratum*, *Punto Tirato*, *Fil Tiré*, drawn work, and Tönder lace. Geometrical designs were used. The threads of the linen were subservient to the pattern. They were preserved in those areas demanding high relief; they were withdrawn or caught together when an open-work effect was required.

ASSEMBLING OF NEEDLEWORK SQUARES Much of the medieval needlework was done in small squares which were easy to handle. These were alternated with squares of plain linen in order to show them up in full effect when large coverings were required for

Needlepoint lace in the making
ABOVE: Working of the design on linen   BELOW: Design on parchment

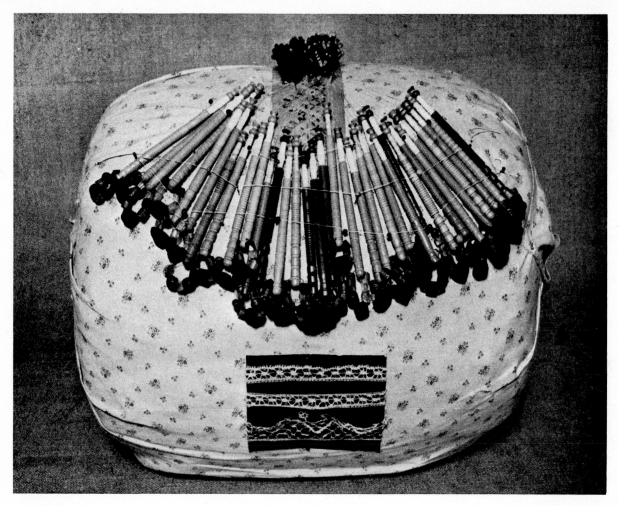

Lace Pillow with Bobbins
in the collection of lace-making instruments in the Welsh Folk Museum, St Fagans

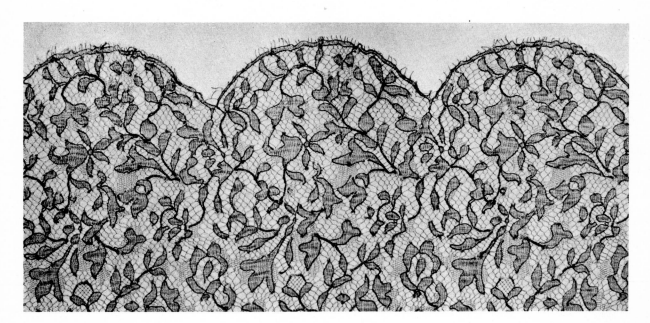

English. Flounce of machine-made lace. Twentieth century

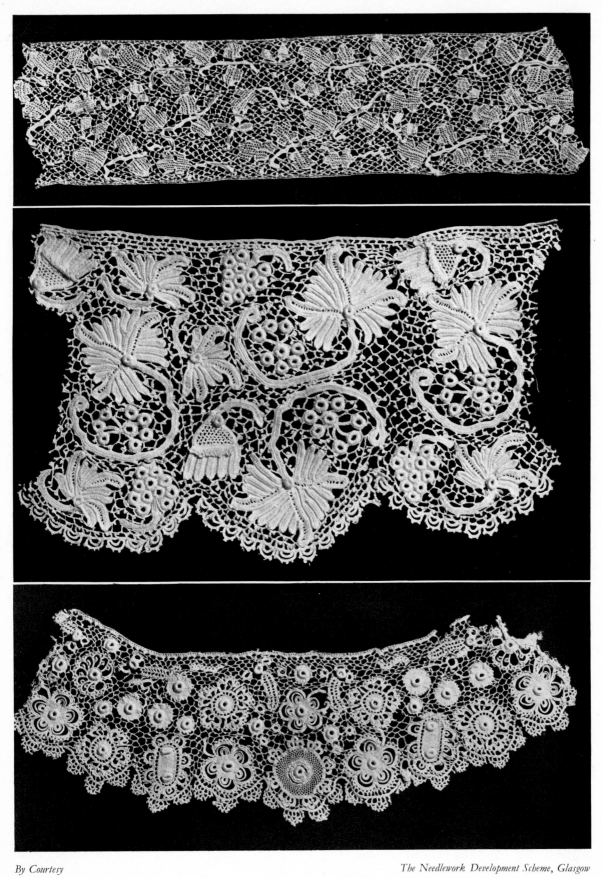

By Courtesy   *The Needlework Development Scheme, Glasgow*

English. Crochet lace. Nineteenth century

ABOVE: Insertion   MIDDLE AND LOWER PANELS: Edgings, showing the use of cotton padding for fillings

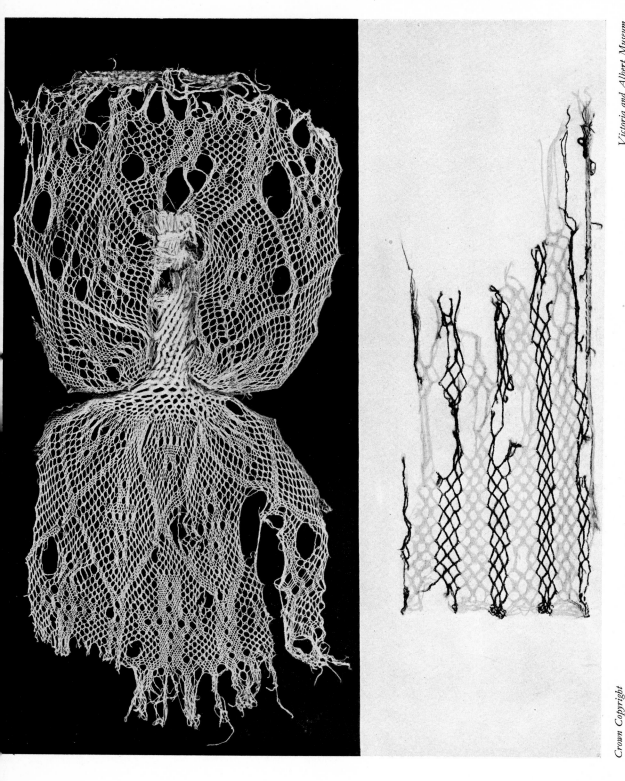

Victoria and Albert Museum

Egypto-Roman netting in linen and woollen threads. From tombs in Egypt

UPPER FRAGMENT found at Khnasya (Herakleopolis Magna) during the excavations of 1903–04. Length: $11\frac{3}{4}$ inches.
Greatest width: $4\frac{1}{4}$ inches

LOWER FRAGMENT from Akhmin (Panopolis), Upper Egypt. Length: $14\frac{1}{2}$ inches. Greatest width: $7\frac{1}{4}$ inches.

bed-curtains and coverlets, curtains and altar hangings. The practice probably spread to personal attire. The *Ballad of Hardyknute* refers to

> An apron set with many a dice
> Of needlework sae rare,
> Wove by nae hand, as ye may guess
> Save that of Fairly fair.

The working of these squares was the amusement of provincial ladies in the later Middle Ages. Their designs portrayed the apostles, angels and saints. The beasts of the Apocalypse, the armorial shields of noble families, monograms, coronets, fleurs-de-lis and *sacrés cœurs* were other patterns created. Cut-work palls were appurtenances of the medieval church; the designs on these included cross bones, death's head, and tears with the sacramental cup.

Needlepoint Lace

Needlepoint lace evolved naturally as a development of open-work embroidery. The foundation of this needlework was a fine linen fabric. When counted threads had been removed and spaces made in the fabric in accordance with a design, the pattern was worked by means of buttonhole stitch or some other close-wrapping stitch. The technique was known in Britain as needlepoint, in France as *point à l'aiguille* and in Italy as *punto in aco*.

PARCHMENT PATTERN As the lace-workers gained in proficiency, the linen foundation was abandoned. Where it did exist, it served merely to carry the design. A practice was soon established of drawing the design in ink upon yellow parchment. This was gummed on to the linen. A single thread was laid on the design and sewn down very closely and carefully to maintain the details and intricacies of the pattern. This process was known as cording. Into this foundation cord, the whole fabric of the cord was worked. When the pattern was completed, the yellow parchment was removed from the linen by means of some sharp instrument and the fastening threads were cut. In this way the lace was set free. In making needlepoint lace, many workers took a technical pride in accomplishing the work with a single needle and thread.

RELIEF INTRODUCED White thread was almost invariably used; coloured, gold and silver threads were used rarely. Gradations of relief were introduced by the needle in elaborate designs. This relief work is seen clearly in exquisite work such as *Gros Point de Venise*. The lace-workers raised the outlines by laying down threads to serve as padding and then working over them. The more expert of the workers were not content until they had emphasized the outlines in double and triple relief. The needle was called on to form varied and ingenious stitches as fillings and as brides or loops linking units of a pattern.

Point laces were very fine and especially so when the brides were formed into part of the pattern. Light meshwork ground supplanted the heavier buttonholing in lace such as

2

the Venetian *Point à Réseau*. France specialized in needlepoint with a *réseau* comprised of hexagonal-shaped brides.

It would be extremely difficult to decide which country achieved the highest standard of excellence in needlepoint lace. Many of the European countries would claim precedence and substantiate their claim by producing wonderful specimens created in the past. Yet most of them would agree in acknowledging the excellence of the needlepoint lace made in Italy in the sixteenth and seventeenth centuries. From the workmanship and the artistic designs of Italian specimens many neighbouring countries drew their real inspiration.

SUPERIORITY OF NEEDLEPOINT Needlepoint was granted a universal prestige above other forms of laces. It was the recognized fabric for state occasions and its higher value was established. Charles Blanc compared the relative merits of needlepoint and bobbin-made lace.

'The dominant character of pillow-made lace', he said, 'is the soft blending of its forms: the needle is to the bobbin what the pencil point is to the stump. The pattern – of which the definition becomes softened when wrought in pillow lace – is depicted with crispness by the needle.'

Crochet

Crochet was known and practised universally in Europe from the sixteenth century onward. The word is derived from the French *crochet* or *croc*, a hook, and the Danish *Krooke* and refers to the hooked tool used.

Crochet lace was made by looping a thread of cotton or silk with this hooked needle to form a design. The worker started with no foundation. The work was done wholly by hand. The thread was looped, pulled through a loop and knotted. Elaborate patterns were made in this way; many of these owed their inspiration to the patterns made in needlepoint and bobbin lace. Some designs had a padded effect achieved through the introduction of a cotton filling which was covered with crochet stitchery.

Crochet lace had the quality of lasting beauty. Unlike many forms of handwork which were exquisite when new but which wore out easily, filet crochet often outlasted the material to which it was applied. The actual technique in crochet work was fairly simple but it required a fair amount of practice before perfection was attained.

In the sixteenth and seventeenth centuries much crochet work was made in nunneries. Lace-work generally was often called nuns' work.

Some of the finest crochet work was called Irish point and much work of fine quality was made in County Monaghan and other centres in Ireland. To meet the demands of crochet workers, many fine cottons were manufactured. Crochet lace enjoyed a great vogue in the Victorian and Edwardian eras when it became fashionable as fancy-work for the leisured classes. Fine designs demanding exacting and intricate workmanship were made and called Irish Point. Other varieties included *Point de Tricot*, Honiton crochet and Raised Rose crochet.

Bobbin Lace

Bobbin lace was made with the aid of pins and pillow; hence the name pillow lace. It was sometimes called bone lace because the bones of fishes and of animals were used both for pins and bobbins.

Before pegs and bobbins were used for making lace, the lace-worker manipulated the thread on her fingers. Sometimes she had to call in the assistance of three or four others in order to have a sufficient number of pegs to complete her work. A Harleian MS. dating from the time of Henry IV of England (1421–1471) shows that small instruments were also employed for making 'Lace Bascon'.

It is a matter of dispute as to whether bobbin lace is older than needlepoint. Many authorities believe that their growth was contemporaneous. Italy and Flanders have each claimed priority in the creation of bobbin lace.

AN OLD LEGEND A pretty legend of Venice tells how a young girl first made bobbin lace in imitation of the pretty coralline known colloquially as mermaid's lace, a gift bestowed on her by her fisherman lover.

SUPERIORITY OF FLEMISH BOBBIN LACES There is no clear evidence as to where bobbin lace originated but Flanders soon established a high reputation for bobbin-work. Seguin wrote: 'As soon as Belgium acquired the art of pillow-making, she unremittingly applied herself to it, and in a short time converted it into a widespread industry, possessing well-merited reputation on account of the delicacy and beauty of its productions. All countries turned to her for them, and she became, as it were, the classic country of pillow lace. Credit for the invention of the special process was readily given to her and no one has since taken the trouble to closely examine her title to it.'

PATTERN BOOKS Bobbin lace was at its best towards the middle of the seventeenth century, a time when needlepoint lace also reached its highest standard of excellence. In the early part of the century Vinciolo and Parrasoli gave special attention to bobbin laces in their pattern books. They gave examples of *merletti a Piombini*, that is, lead bobbin laces, and stated under their designs the number of bobbins required. Patterns of bobbin laces had, however, appeared as early as 1596. Two patterns of bobbin lace suitable for ornamenting household linen appeared in Giacomo Franco's *Nuovo Inventione*.

The quality of bobbin lace improved with the advance of the lace-worker in the degree of precision with which the bobbins were thrown and twisted. The plaiting and twisting of the threads was a characteristic of bobbin lace and was a distinguishing feature.

During the seventeenth century, the bobbin workers invariably turned to the needlepoint laces of the period for their patterns. *Gros Point de Venise* was copied on an extensive scale.

FINE SPECIMENS OF BOBBIN LACE Among the more celebrated of bobbin laces was that made at Mechlin. In accordance with a custom prevalent at the time, the Mechlin lace-workers sent around to neighbouring countries pedlars equipped with lace boxes. One lace edging was known as *Trolle Kant;* it was in the nature of a sampler showing the various patterns which the Mechlin workers were prepared to create. This lace sampler proved to be one of the most popular of edgings. The bobbin lace-workers of Brussels also achieved renown. They specialized in fine work. The mesh of their *réseau* was hexagonal in shape. In Britain the bobbin laces of Buckinghamshire became celebrated in the eighteenth century.

Bobbin lace was known in France as *dentelle à fuseau* and in Italy as *merli a piombini;* these terms came into international use among lace-workers. Flemish lace-workers, in particular, favoured this method of lace-making; their term for it was *spelle werke.*

USE OF THE TERM 'POINT' It is well to safeguard against the confusion sometimes wrought in the study of lace owing to the prefix *point* made with reference to certain pillow laces; for instance, *Point de Malines* and *Point de Valenciennes.* These are not needlepoint laces; they are bobbin-made. Further confusion has occurred at times through the use of the term *point* with reference to a particular stitch in lace-making as in *Point de Paris* and *Point de Neige.*

TECHNIQUE EMPLOYED As with needlepoint lace, the pattern for bobbin lace was drawn on parchment or 'roller'. Ample supplies of thread were wound round the bobbins attached to the pillow. The technique of working was elaborate, involving the passing and plaiting of threads. The work demanded much skill, though the ease and dexterity with which the pillow lace-workers manipulated the pins and bobbins seemed to belie the statement. Each bobbin was worked independently and the thread was passed around the pins stuck in the pillow. Several lace-workers making patterns independently made them in uniformity. The various parts were easily united to make up a wide portion of lace.

Pillows and their Accessories

TYPES OF CUSHIONS AND THEIR SEVERAL USES Pillows were made in great variety. Some were cylindrical, others had flat bases. Some were pyramid-shaped and some were square. Many lace-workers used small flat cushions on which they made single ornaments and flowers for appliqué lace. Portuguese lace-workers used cushions on basket stands which they held between their feet. In Spain long cushions were used. Makers of silk laces in Bayeux and Northern France used big cushions capable of taking as many as six hundred bobbins.

Each type of cushion had its special uses. A collar or head-dress or some article requiring repeats of a design was best worked on a rotating cylinder. The use of a flat cushion facilitated the working of filings and elaborate stitching for the lace-worker was able to spread out the threads in all directions. A large piece of lace was not suitable for flat cushion work for when one section was finished the worker was obliged to take out all the pins before commencing on a further section.

Since the accessories used in the making of pillow lace attract the collector almost as strongly as do actual specimens of old lace, some reference to the charming bobbins and jingles used in the making of bobbin laces is justified.

BOBBIN The bobbins used were small elongated spindles. They were reels holding the thread. They were bulbous at one end for ease of manipulation. Their size varied according to the thickness of the thread used. Bobbins used for guipure and torchon laces were large because of the heavy thread used. Fine fabrics like Mechlin and Valenciennes laces called for superfine thread and light, thin bobbins. Local characteristics crept into the bobbins. Those used in Normandy were of white wood; they were very straight, without a neck and bore a shield of horn called a *noquette* to ensure that the thread was kept clean. The lace-makers of Auvergne also fitted this device on their bobbins. They favoured bone bobbins of many sizes with long, thick-set necks. Flemish workers used bobbins of wood, dark and highly polished. These were turned attractively and were usually slender in shape. Danish bobbins were also prettily turned and were fitted with rings of gaily-coloured beads. Portuguese bobbins were of an attractive shape and were mellow with time and use.

The old lace bobbins were seldom bought in the shops. Like the actual art of making pillow lace, they were handed down as heirlooms in families.

Some of the most attractive bobbins of Britain date from the Queen Anne period. There are others, too, of earlier date. Many of the bobbins used were of boxwood. They were small and light for they were used to make exquisite lace of gossamer thread. When coarser thread was used in lace-making, bead spangles were fastened to the edge of the bobbins. The main purpose of these beads was to weight the bobbin so as to keep it in place on the pillow; but they served for ornament also.

In order to preserve the thread from injury, the bobbins were made from closely-grained wood. Dark bobbins were made from ebony, plum and damson; light bobbins were made from apple, oak, maple and spindle-wood. When the bobbins were fashioned in bone, they were dyed in many colours and were weighted with beads, pewter, copper and brass.

SPECIAL TYPES OF BOBBINS One of the oldest forms was that known as the 'bitted bobbin'. This had an elegant shape and was usually made of dark wood. A pattern was inserted in light wood. The 'tinsey bobbin' was of wood or bone; it received this name because small pieces of tin were let into the main body to form a design. Most of the patterns were very pretty and many were curious. The 'hip-bobbin' received its name from its elegant shape and slim waist. The 'wire bobbin' had fine wire twisted around the wood. Metal rings were attached to some bobbins and served to hold the thread or gimp. Sometimes bobbins were made in three sections, two being of wood and one of bone, each fitting closely into the other.

INSCRIPTIONS Of peculiar interest were the names and mottoes carved on bobbins. Sometimes the initials of a husband and wife were interwoven to form a puzzle on the face of a bobbin. Many a 'John', 'Thomas', 'William', 'Owen' and 'Giles' created, through

2*

succeeding generations, yards and yards of fine lace. Women's names were often inscribed and an assembly of bobbins often formed a calendar of the lace-worker's life, each bobbin commemorating some special event. The motto bobbin was ubiquitous: 'Let no false lover gaine my heart'; 'To me, my deare, you may come near.' Bobbins commemorated events of personal importance: 'George Read, died February 19 1832 aged 6 months.' Sometimes the collector of today comes across a bobbin bearing some historical reference – to the death of Queen Adelaide, a patroness of lace-making, or to the death of Nelson, a national hero.

BOBBIN SPANGLES A complete set of spangles attached to a bobbin consisted of nine beads. The two 'top beads' were usually a pair, set one on each side; the six beads which followed, divided into three each side, were called 'square cuts'. The centre beads were red and were set among white beads. The 'bottom bead' was the most important and was, in turn, weighted with a thimble, a baby's tooth or some foreign gewgaw.

The old beads forming the spangles retained their charm through many years. Some beads were clear; some were mottled. Some were of glass; others were of china. The fragrance of romance still clings to many a 'bottom bead', weighted with keys and seals, with rings and with tassels from a soldier's uniform or with the 'luckiest' of keepsakes, the bottom button from a sweetheart's waistcoat.

BOBBIN PINS The pins used in the making of pillow lace were often curious. Originally they were of bone, usually fish bones; later they were of thorns or wood and then of brass with removable caps. These brass pins were pushed half their length into the pillow and beads of various colours were put on. The colours of the beads facilitated the working of the design. Burrs from the hedgerows were the traditional pin caps in some districts. They were gathered and placed in the sun to dry; they were then put into a brass thimble with vinegar and salt. Alternatively, they were smoked in damp hay placed in the cottage chimney. When placed on the pins, the burrs dried; they shrank into shape and tightened.

Machine-made Lace

Machine-made lace is, more accurately speaking, machine-made net. The advent of this type ousted to a considerable degree hand-made lace, for it was cheap and plentiful and within easy reach of all classes of society.

In the early stages of development, machine-made lace was created on looms which were operated by hand; later, looms were operated by power.

ENGLISH ENTERPRISE IN MACHINE-MADE FABRICS Britain claimed a leading part in the development of machine-made lace and France followed her closely.

Cycles of development are apparent in the development of machine processes. It was in the year 1798 that net was first made by machinery. The year 1809 marked a distinct advance; machine bobbin net was invented. In 1837, what was known as the Jacquard system, was applied to the bobbin-net machine.

One of the prime inventors of a machine capable of making an open-work mesh was a man named Hammond, a stocking framework knitter of Nottingham. The loop net machines were in essence a development of the stocking machine. The principles underlying the working involved the removal of prescribed loops from one set of needles to an adjoining set and the creation of small holes in the fabric. Hammond's machine (1768) and kindred machines produced a kind of knitted lace comprised of running loops and stitches, resembling closely that which was to be known later as 'Brussels ground'.

In 1777, two Nottingham men introduced what was called 'the pin'. This point net machine was so called because of the sharp points or 'pin' fitted into it. Improvements in point net followed rapidly and several varieties such as 'barley-corn', 'square' and 'spider net' were available. An open stitch, known as 'Derby rib' was also much in demand. This had been invented for a stocking machine by Jedediah Strutt as early as 1758.

Despite all the improvements and new stitches, net was as yet only a kind of knitting. The process involved was that of passing a single thread from one part of the frame to another. Any break in the thread meant an unravelling of the work. As a precaution against such breakages, the thread was stiffened with gum; this introduced stiffness and solidity into the net. When the warp or chain machine was invented breakages were less frequent. In this machine the processes employed by the knitter and the weaver were united. Many people claimed a share in its invention, and it is difficult to legislate among the claimants.

HEATHCOAT'S INVENTION Much patience and ingenuity were spent to improve Hammond's invention in order to create a ground of pillow lace. John Heathcoat, of Leicestershire, succeeded in creating a skilfully contrived bobbin-net machine. He called it 'Old Loughborough'. The term 'bobbin-net' was used because the threads were wound round bobbins. At first, net a little more than an inch wide was made. Later this was advanced to a yard and then to three yards.

The social historian finds romance and drama revolving around Heathcoat's bobbin-net machines. In that wave of vandalism known as the Luddite Riots (1811), twenty-seven of Heathcoat's machines were destroyed. The year 1823 witnessed what was termed the 'bobbin net fever', for Heathcoat's patent expired in that year and many people, drawn from all sections of society, were moved by a desire to have the legal use of net machines in the hope of getting rich quickly. Vast quantities of bobbin net were made; consequently, prices fell. Nottingham remained, however, the main centre of supply and the net created there took precedence over the finely-finished, machine-made products of France and the Netherlands.

France took a practical and early interest in the manufacture of machine-made lace since 1778, when Caillon succeeded in manufacturing a kind of *tricot dentelle*. True to tradition, royal patronage came to the assistance of industry and art in France. The Duc de Liancourt was sent by Louis XIV to England to observe the latest improvements made in stocking and net machinery. Any progress on the part of France was, however, negatived by the breakdown of commercial intercourse between England and France during the Revolutionary and Napoleonic periods.

SMUGGLING OF NET AND OF MACHINERY Napoleon prohibited the buying of English-made nets, but so strong was the desire for it that bales of Nottingham net were smuggled into France. Knowledge of this led to very deliberate efforts to obtain bobbin-net machines from England. The English Government retaliated by making stringent laws against the export of English machinery. Strict vigilance was kept at the Channel ports and on the Nottingham factories. Nevertheless bobbin-net machines of the English type came into use in France. According to tradition, a man named Cutts, a workman who had been employed by Heathcoat, took a machine to Valenciennes in 1815. He set up a similar machine at Douai in 1816. Soon bobbin net was being manufactured in France on a spectacular scale. Calais became a thriving centre for machine-made lace. In 1816, a man named James Clark introduced an English machine into the town, having smuggled it across the Channel with the aid of French sailors. French lace-workers were soon improving the machine-made net by embroidering it by hand.

BELGIAN PRE-EMINENCE IN MACHINE LACE Belgium had long coveted the use of bobbin-net machines. By 1834 she had succeeded in obtaining possession of eight machines which were set up at Brussels. These manufactured double and twisted net. On these nets pillow-made flowers and ornamentations were sewn. The net was of very fine ground and was soon to achieve international renown as 'Brussels net'. Ghent and Alost, St Fosse and Termonde were other thriving centres and Belgium soon achieved pre-eminence for machine-made lace and surpassed both England and France in the production of it.

TECHNIQUE OF DECORATING BOBBIN NET A distinction gradually arose between workers in machine bobbin net and machine-made lace. England clung tenaciously to her claim to the invention of bobbin net. France applied the Jacquard system to the net frame and consequently claimed the invention of machine lace.

Flounces and shawls of the latter half of the nineteenth century were in 'run lace'. The pattern which was to be run was printed by means of an engraved block and the ground was stretched on a frame. The lace-worker was known as the 'lace-runner'. She supported the net with her left hand and followed the lines of the pattern with her right. The filling-in of flowers and leaves was known as 'open-working' or 'fining'.

Bobbin net had many of the characteristics of bobbin lace. In 1820 a Nottingham man named Symes invented a pattern called 'Grecian net'. This was popular until it was supplanted by the spot pattern or '*point d'esprit*'. Various fancy nets such as buttonhole and tatting followed in rapid succession.

French laces were complex in pattern and of fine texture. The Calais lace-workers emulated those of Valenciennes. They manufactured a square-grounded mesh. Popular, too, were the *dentelles de laine* of Le Puy, the black and white blonde laces of Calais and the fine nets of complex character made there.

STITCHERY OF APPLIQUÉ LACE Sewing and stitching machines were improved upon and these were used for the enhancement of machine-made lace. Among the many and varied stitches made by these early machines were the 'overlock' and 'Bonnaz' and those used for what was known as 'Cornelly embroidery'. Decorative stitches were applied to a form of cut-work by means of which an opaque fabric was placed over net. The nature of the foundation fabric determined the form and treatment of the design. Stitchery was applied to the outlines only of the pattern in some laces; elsewhere, stitchery was used as a filling. When the design had been treated, all superfluous material was removed so that the net foundation was fully revealed.

ARTISTIC VALUE OF HAND-MADE LACES Old hand-made laces were copied by machine and many of the replicas were admirable. Profusion of machine-made lace and bobbin net resulted in increasing the value of hand-made specimens and, consequent on this, collectors have sought out yet more eagerly the exquisite laces of the past. M. Didron, in his *Report on the Decorative Arts at the Universal Exhibition of 1878*, referred to the cheap machine-made substitutes of hand-made lace and said: 'Cheapness is never commendable in respect of things which are not absolute necessities; it lowers artistic standard. Lace must inevitably lose the best features of its delight for us, on the day that it ceases to be precious and relatively rare.'

RUSKIN ON HAND-MADE LACE Ruskin, that veteran champion of aesthetic worth, has written: 'There is still some distinction between machine-made and hand-made lace. I will suppose that distinction so far done away with that, a pattern once invented, you can spin lace as you now do thread.

'Everybody then might wear not only lace collars but lace gowns. Do you think that when everybody can wear them, everybody would be proud of wearing them?

'A spider may perhaps be rationally proud of his own cobweb, even though all the fields in the morning are covered with the like, for he made it himself; but suppose a machine spun it for him. Suppose all the gossamer were Nottingham made. If you think of it, you will find the whole value of lace as a possession depends on the fact of its having BEAUTY which has been the reward of industry and attention.

'That the thing itself is a price – a thing everybody cannot have; that it proves by the look of it, the ability of the maker; that it proves by the rarity of it, the dignity of its wearer – either that she must have been so industrious as to save money which can buy, say, a piece of jewellery, of gold tissue, or of fine lace – or else that she is a noble person to whom her neighbours concede as an honour the privilege of wearing finer dress than they.

'If they all choose to have lace too – if it ceases to be a price, it becomes, does it not, only a cobweb. The real good of a piece of lace then, you will find, is that it should show first, that the designer of it had a pretty fancy; next that the maker of it had fine fingers; lastly that the wearer of it had worthiness or dignity enough to obtain what is difficult to obtain and common sense enough not to wear it on all occasions.'

The Identification of Lace

The identification and exact classification of lace is often a difficult task. Throughout the centuries, there was a ready interchange in the technique and styles favoured by the lace-makers of different countries. Photographs of lace serve to reveal interesting features but the study of actual specimens with the aid of a magnifying glass brings a richer and truer reward.

TEXTURE OF FABRIC The amateur begins by learning to distinguish broadly between the more general types of lace. Certain well-defined characteristics are easily assimilated. The groundwork or *réseau* of pillow-made lace is made of threads which have been twisted or plaited. The *réseau* of needlepoint lace is made of buttonhole stitching. Machine-made net on which lace embroideries have been applied are easy to distinguish. The *réseau* is hard and stiff to the touch, it refuses to roll up under pressure from the fingers in the silky-supple response of hand-made lace. The meticulous accuracy of the mesh reflects machine process. The mesh of hand-made lace, even in the finest specimens, varies considerably.

MIXED LACES When classifying lace, recognition must be made of the existence of *mixed* laces. These seem to baffle too minute a classification. The *réseau* is made on the pillow and the pattern or *toile* with the needle, or the alternative order may obtain.

THREADS OF DIFFERENT VARIETIES The threads of needlepoint lace do not unravel easily for the knots impede action. The threads of bobbin-made lace can be unravelled but the process is tedious because of the plaiting. Machine-made lace will, however, unravel easily and with a continuous flow. The number of threads in the unravelled portion serve as a distinguishing clue. In needlepoint there is a single thread only; in bobbin lace there are several.

The *date* of manufacture is an important factor. The unravelling of threads will provide useful information. If a thread of about twenty inches is unravelled, it can be examined for joins. If the thread reveals no joinings, it is probable that the work dates from the early nineteenth century onward. Thread prepared by machine has few joins. Hand-prepared thread had, of necessity, many joinings occasioned by the limitations of the spinner using her distaff.

PATTERNS A CLUE TO DATE OF MANUFACTURE *Design* is another important factor in tracing the date of a specimen. Geometrical designs were usual in the sixteenth century. The sampler work of the period proved less of a source of information than an end in itself. The angularity of the designs is noticeable in especial in the working of petals, leaves and other motifs demanding a more natural and rounded treatment.

The patterns of the seventeenth century were more ambitious. Backgrounds were dispensed with. Lace-workers concentrated on the working of scroll patterns which were linked together and supported by tie-bars, known technically as brides or bridges. These tie-bars are particularly fine in needlepoint lace, being made of one or two threads, button-holed over closely. These brides are in themselves a clue to the date of a specimen. They first appeared in the fifteenth century, at first in a plain form and later ornamented with a knot or dot. The tie-bars of the sixteenth century had a single or double loop. Those of the seventeenth century bore a star motif.

The bar joinings of fifteenth-century lace-work were in a simple V-shape. In the succeeding centuries, it was usual to make a looped bar to intersect the V. In the second half of the seventeenth century, the barettes were unsymmetrical and uneven.

The seventeenth-century lace-workers introduced into the main design picots or *fleurs volantes*. These were diamond shaped and worked round a raised cordonnet.

A certain uniformity characterized eighteenth-century designs. There was a pronounced tendency to balance all details symmetrically. Lace designs imitated very closely those created on silk and linen fabrics. Stylistic and naturalistic patterns strove together in close rivalry amid an array of festoons, garlands and bouquets.

When machine-made lace appeared, designers gave greater attention to the mesh background. It was given greater prominence and became more elaborate. Over-elaboration of design set in and the later years of the nineteenth century witnessed a continuous decadence. The processed fabric proved to be an unsuitable medium for the ultra-naturalistic patterns created upon it.

The edging or *couronne* of a lace may indicate its age. Angular points edged the laces of the Middle Ages. A softer note was introduced by the rounded scallops of the sixteenth century. In the seventeenth century, the scallop was ornamented with a dot. In the following century it was usual to alternate a large scallop with a small one and ornament each with a small dot in the centre.

USE AND SIGNIFICANCE OF 'ENGRÊLURES' *Engrêlures*, footings or headings, also varied with the centuries. These were narrow laces which were attached to the upper edge of a flounce or of a border of lace. Their purpose was to preserve the actual flounce from injury when it was sewn to the main foundation of a garment. The *engrêlure* in itself is unsafe evidence of date of manufacture for, being subject to hard wear, it was sometimes renewed, and the renewed portion was of a later date than the main flounce. Flax thread was used for making old hand-made *engrêlures*, but those made by machine were of cotton thread. The rules regulating tie-bars applied to footings as well as to the main fabric. The earliest footings were simply a series of crossed bars. These were ornamented with knots and picots as the lace-workers grew more expert.

It is sometimes difficult to decide on the country of origin. The lace-workers migrated to different countries taking with them their patterns and special methods. Innovations crept in and these were deliberately fostered when it was realized that the orientation was establishing a new vogue.

UNITS OF DESIGN The actual units of lace patterns are an indication of the time of working. Lace patterns of the medieval period are true to type, comprising the representation of sacred animals, symbolic groups, trees, figures and monsters. All lines are hard and stiff; rounded effects are absent. A unit was repeated again and again. At first, lace was joined by straight lines only and uniform repetition was necessary. The lace-workers of the sixteenth century discovered another method of joining and this gave scope for the introduction of rounded motifs as well as angular ones.

Geometrical patterns comprised of squares, circles, triangles, were used freely until the middle of the seventeenth century. Gradually, the flowing lines of the Renaissance designs were asserting themselves; these included scroll patterns, wreaths, festoons and garlands. These were unified into compact designs which were linked together with brides or bridges.

In the eighteenth century, rococo styles grew popular. The ungraceful patterns, fantastic attributes, stiff forms and unwieldy bouquets were accepted. A marked decadence in design set in.

Towards the end of the eighteenth century there grew up an inclination to dispense with formal designs. The Dotted style was accepted. Lace specimens of this period are powdered with dots and sprigs, with tears, rosettes and insects.

THE LACES OF ITALY

THE decrees of fashion in the fifteenth and sixteenth centuries resulted in the extensive use of lace. The demand brought about an increase of interest among the lace-workers and a greater supply was ensured.

PROSPERITY OF ITALIAN CITIES The Renaissance era witnessed a great vogue for Italian laces; money poured in from all European countries into the treasure chests of Venice, Milan, Genoa, Florence and other cities, making the citizens rich and prosperous. One of the prime ambassadors of Italian lace-craft was the handsome Medici collar, so named because the Italian-born French Queen, Catherine de Medici favoured it. Venetian points of exquisite workmanship formed its main trimming and gros point was used when heavy collars were required.

The beauty of Italian lace-work was established at an early period. Many competent judges regarded Italian work as unrivalled. Fine needlepoint lace was being made in the fifteenth century. During the sixteenth century it was one of the main occupations of the convents. One of the oldest paintings depicting the use of lace is a portrait of a lady by Carpaccio and dated 1523. Edgings of lace trim the cuffs of the lady's dress. The design of the lace was probably common at the time and it was to find a place in the pattern book of Vecellio when this was published some eighty years later.

CHURCH LACE Much lace was required for ecclesiastical purposes and the splendour of the Roman Catholic Church inspired the lace-worker. Devoted women spent many years making laces to adorn the vestments of the priests, the cope, the surplice, the tunic, the veil, the stole, the chasuble, the dalmatic, the amice, the alb, the girdle and cassock. Guipure laces were made for altar hangings and for veils for the Host. Laces were made to adorn the many statues within the churches.

In the early stages of the Renaissance, the term 'lace' had a wide connotation for it included *passement* and *dentelle*. At a period when elaborate velvet costumes were favoured by men and women alike, *passement* was used lavishly as a trimming. *Dentelle* referred to early needlepoint and bobbin lace. *Passement* was made of a broad flat braid or gimp and gold, silver or metallic thread was used in the making of it.

WIDE CONNOTATION OF THE TERM 'LACE' The elaborate dress of the sixteenth century occasioned the prosperity of the lace-maker's art. Venice appears to have been dubious of the true worth of its success at the commencement of the lace industry. The officers of the Republic issued several ordinances prohibiting under pain of heavy fines the wearing of *punto in aria* in towns. A sumptuary law of 1514 limited the use of lace in 'ladies' cloaks, laces, gloves embroidered with gold and silk embroideries generally, fans, gondolas, sedan chairs'.

EXTRAVAGANT USE OF LACE The demand for lace continued, however, and so successful did the lace-makers of Italy become that, at an early stage in the history of the lace industry, they were exporting large quantities of their work to many of the European countries and in particular to the royal court of France. The demand for needlepoint increased steadily so that in the reign of Louis XIII courtiers were wearing it to an extravagant degree. Rank and wealth were signalled by the amount of lace used on collars, cuffs, knee garters, the tops of gloves and of boots and on the silken scarves worn diagonally across the body.

RETICELLA WORK The high standard which the Italian workers attained did not confuse them concerning the necessity both to maintain and better their achievements. In reticella work, only the very finest cloths were used and accuracy of workmanship was sought meticulously. No effort was spared in the counting of threads and in their grouping. In the cloisters of the convents, in the halls of the nobility, in the lace schools of the proletariat, the finest craftsmanship obtained.

GEOMETRIC PATTERNS The earliest Venetian reticella work shows the popularity of geometrical patterns. At first this work had been called Gothic Point or Greek Lace, but gradually the term reticella was established. By tradition, the Italian needle-workers were accustomed to coloured embroidery. When the lace-workers wearied of the geometric patterns, they reverted to the past to seek inspiration for new designs. The beautiful and intricate scrolls and festoons which had decorated the missals and psalteries of the medieval church were developed to serve as designs for reticella work. Other designs incorporated those already well established in the Levant through the skilful hands of the Moorish and Eastern leather-workers and tapestry-workers.

A decided advance was soon made in technique also. The linen foundation depreciated in value; in so far as was possible, it was abandoned. Reticella work continued to increase in popularity. Sumptuary laws regulating the use of gold and silver thread gave it a further fillip. Interest became focused on the charm and beauty of white work.

PUNTO TAGLIATO A close rival in popularity was that form of needlework known in Italy as *punto tagliato* (punto=stitch; tag=cut). This, like early reticella, was worked on a linen foundation. Rectangular spaces were made in the linen by the withdrawal of warp and weft threads. These spaces were filled in with fine needlwork. On this foundation of stitchery a design in the form of a scroll or garland of flowers was worked. The working of this superimposed design was termed *punto in aria*. This type of lace was faithfully recorded for future generations by the Venetian school of portrait painters.

PUNTO IN ARIA In 1542 a book of designs giving guidance and inspiration for *punto in aria* was published by a Venetian pattern maker, Mattheo Pagan. Pattern books for lace-making were not numerous. It was the practice to copy designs from samplers which were far less expensive than books. There were, however, several editions of pattern books. The South Kensington Museum possesses patterns by Vinciolo, Vicellio and Isabella Parasole.

Another type of Italian cut-work was that termed *intagliata*. Here also, the main principle was the removal of threads in a linen cloth and the filling in of the spaces created with geometric patterns, arabesques and fruits. The patterns in this variety of cut-work were much more ambitous than in other types. Workers of *intagliata* were happy only when all the spaces in the linen had been filled completely with conventional cut-work designs, with heraldic devices, and, later, with human and animal forms.

Technique was of a high standard and gradually the needle-workers began to regard the linen foundation of their work not as a framework but as a redundancy. After successful experimenting, the old system of using a linen cloth was abandoned. Instead, a cloth-backed parchment on which the design had been traced was used. A fine thread was couched closely along the outline of the design; the stitchery of the lace-work was then made on the *surface* of the parchment. The couched thread of the pattern served as a framework on which to hang the looped stitches of the actual lace. When the surplus material had been cut away, the beauty of the design was evident.

As lace-workers attained greater dexterity, they became more ambitious in their designs. Geometrical designs were now abandoned or were merely incorporated as accessories to the main design. Deep points and foliated scrolls were now favoured.

USE OF THE CORDONNET Contemporaneous with this advance in technique and design, there was an ever-increasing demand for fine and elaborate lace. This was required as a trimming for the rich fabrics, cloth, velvet, brocade and silk which were being used for costume. Largely in answer to this demand, *punto in aria* orientated in form and began to incorporate a well-defined *cordonnet*. This was a raised cord which served to outline the design. There were alternative methods of working this *cordonnet*. Some workers covered the cord with fine buttonhole stitching in gossamer thread before attaching it to the outline of the design; other workers preferred a method involving the covering of the cord with buttonhole stitch and applying it to the design, all in one process. An excellent use of *cordonnet* was made in raised Venetian point. It introduced high relief into the pattern and it was usually edged with fine picots. The use of the *cordonnet* was soon practised by most of the lace-workers of Europe for *Point de Venise* was for long the most popular of European laces.

PUNTO ROSELLINE In the eighteenth century there was a further development of Italian needlepoint lace. *Punto roselline* or rose point established for itself a European reputation. Fine workmanship and delicacy of design were its main characteristics. It received its name from the tiny roses or stars worked in every available space on the design. Such was the enthusiasm of the workers that they superimposed stars upon stars and created them on the brides as well as on the actual designs. This variety of lace was often referred to as *Point de Neige*, for the heavy showers of white roses or stars were reminiscent of a snowfall.

POINT DE VENISE À RÉSEAU Surpassing *Point de Venise* and *Point roselline* in fine workmanship was yet another variety of Italian needlepoint; this was known as *Point de Venise à réseau*. But few specimens have been preserved and these are sought after zealously by connoisseurs. A flat point was worked on a ground of needlepoint; characteristic of this ground was the working of the mesh to follow the lines and curves of the pattern instead of forming the threads to lie horizontally and vertically without cognizance of the lines of the design.

PEASANT LACE Many beautiful peasant laces were made in Italy. These bore traditional designs. *Punto avorio* made in the Valle Vogna of Northern Italy involved the uniting of bands of silk and of linen as well as actual lace-work.

DECLINE OF ITALIAN LACES The lace industry of Italy decayed when that of France grew prosperous. Colbert, the astute minister of Louis XIV, encouraged Italian lace-workers to settle in France in order to foster the lace industry of that country. The French soon proved themselves to be apt pupils. The large supplies of Italian lace were no longer imported, for the French were able to manufacture their own. Moreover, they were called on to supply other nations of Europe when they showed that they were capable of producing such beautiful laces as their renowned *Point de France*.

Italian Needlepoint Lace

Venetian Needlepoint

Venice stands out pre-eminently among all centres manufacturing needlepoint lace. She was primarily responsible for teaching the art of needlepoint to the other countries of Europe. One can only surmise at this juncture as to where she learnt the art of needlepoint. There is much evidence to support the theory that she learnt many of the rudiments from the Saracens who had settled in Italy.

VENICE THE CENTRE OF FASHION IN THE MIDDLE AGES Throughout the Middle Ages, Venice was not only a focal point of trade; she was also the centre of fashion for all the courts of Europe. Not only did she supply silks and satins and brocades and laces together with many other articles of adornment and luxury, but she also decreed their mode of use. Not until the late Middle Ages did she give way to Paris as a centre of fashion.

WIDE USE OF VENICE LACE The medieval wardrobe accounts of England signify the wide use of lace from Venice. 'Fringe of Venice and mantle laces of white silk and Venice

Collar of needlepoint lace
Venice. Gros Point de Venise. *Seventeenth century*
High relief is introduced to emphasize details on heavy needlepoint lace

Italy. Three borders of reticella lace. Late sixteenth century

Flounce of needlepoint lace
Italian. Point flat de Venise. Second half of the seventeenth century
Length: 9 feet.   Depth: 22 inches

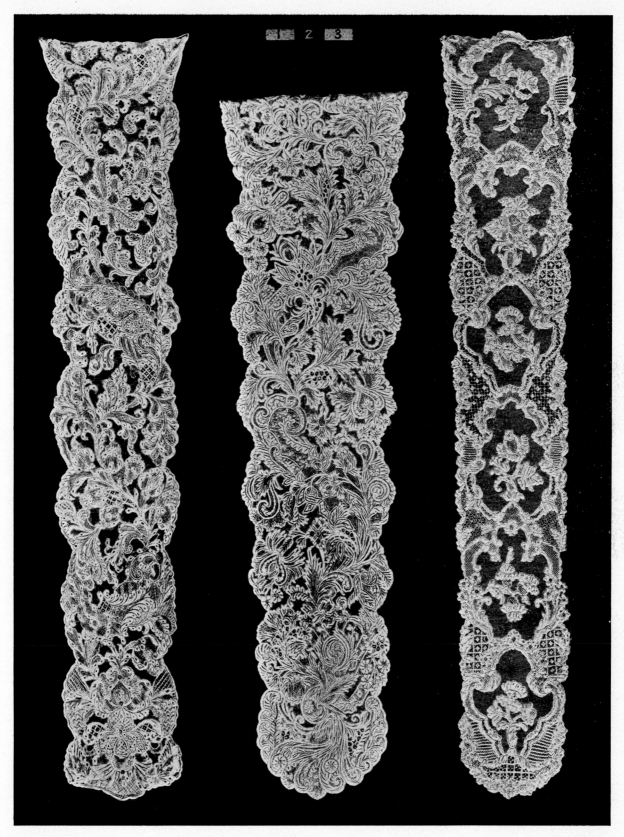

Lappets in needlepoint lace
Venice. Point de Venise à réseau. *First half of the eighteenth century*
A needlepoint lace of the greatest delicacy

gold', were used at the coronation of Richard III. There are also references to 'partlets knit caul-fashion of Venice gold'. Elizabeth of York purchased 'gold of Venice and other necessaries'. In the Tudor period, Italian cut-work and Venice lace were purchased on a generous scale.

Catherine de Medici took with her to France collars of rich point lace. Their popularity was immediate. Frenchmen and others sent to Venice for large supplies of Italian needle-point which came to be known for a period as *Point de Medicis*.

VARIETIES OF VENETIAN LACE Reticella, or Greek lace, *punto intagliato*, or cut-work, *punto in aria*, an open lace or guipure, were among the more usual varieties sought. Much favoured for household furnishings was *punto in maglia*, a form of darned netting, and also *punto à groppo*, knotted lace in thick thread.

Most celebrated of all, however, was a variety which was practised at a time when the lace industry of Venice had already begun to decline in the seventeenth century. This was the famous *Punto Tagliato à Fogliami*. It was worked on a parchment pattern, the mesh net-work ground being abandoned. The units of the design were linked with bars. By means of padding threads, the outlines of the pattern were shown in high relief. Double and triple relief were introduced into some of the most treasured specimens such as the Rose or Raised Venetian Point and the *Gros Point de Venise*. Designs were conventional comprising flowers, festoons and scrolls. Some of this lace was made in silk; most of it was in natural or cream colour but some was in yellow, blue or purple. Portrait painters did full honour to these laces and delighted in portraying them in their many intricacies.

VENICE INSPIRES FRANCE When Colbert established lace manufactories in France, he turned to Venice for guidance. Monseigneur de Bonzy, Bishop of Biers, was the French ambassador in Venice. His communications to Colbert throw light on the prosperity of Venice: 'All the convents and poor families make a living of this lace-making . . . I see how easy it would be for you to establish the making of Venetian needlepoint laces in France, if you were to send over here a few of the best French lace-makers' daughters to be taught, so that in time they should impart their instruction to others in France.'

Of the convents mentioned that of San Zaccaria was the most famed for its needle-point laces. In 1673 Colbert wrote to the new French ambassador in Venice, M. le Comte d'Avaux: 'I have gladly received the collar of needlepoint lace worked in relief that you have sent me and I find it very beautiful. I shall have it compared with those now being made by our own lace-makers, although I may tell you beforehand that as good specimens are now made in this Kingdom.'

DECLINE OF VENETIAN LACE Colbert's enterprise and his establishment of a lace factory at Alençon together with the rise of the fine needlepoint laces of Brussels resulted in the decline of Venetian lace. She adapted herself to the changed times. The lace-workers realized that men wore less lace as women wore them the more, and concentrated on laces of finer texture. They abandoned the heavy scrolls and rich reliefs for the more graceful branches of Rose Point designs.

BURANO LACE Efforts were made to create needlepoint laces with meshed grounds. At Burano, an island five miles north of Venice, meshed grounds were made with single threads. The mesh of the groundwork did not follow the curves of the pattern. The whole bore a handsome effect, achieved unintentionally perhaps and due to the fact that the thread used was spun unevenly.

Point d'Argentella

Much indecision exists as to the true origin of this lace. Many authorities declare it to be the work of French lace-workers; others locate it at Venice and others at Genoa where lace-workers were said to be endeavouring to copy *Point d'Alençon*. If this was so, then the lace-workers of Genoa achieved the creation of a new type of lace. *Point d'Argentella* resembled *Point d'Alençon* very closely but there were distinguishing features. Characteristic of it were the well-defined partridge-eye ground, the numerous finely-worked *jours*, or fillings, and the mayflower pattern.

This lace represented in part a gesture of the Italian needlepoint workers to create a light lace of fine fabric when heavy points had become *démodé*. They made no effort to emphasize the outline but kept it flat. Many of the Argentella laces are *semes* or powderings, featuring circles, ovals and sprigs upon net grounds. Because of the whiteness of the thread used and the grace of the designs many preferred *Point d'Argentella* to Brussels lace.

Italian Bobbin Laces
Genoa

Genoa and Milan were the two main centres of pillow lace in Italy. It was the custom to copy the least complicated of the needlepoint laces or to adapt them for the use of pillow-makers. Skilful pattern designers, among them being Isabella Catena Parasole, later created patterns for pillow laces and indicated under them the number of bobbins required for working.

As early as the mid-nineteenth century, Genoa was a flourishing centre producing *passamenteries* and lace in gold thread.

The English wardrobe accounts of the sixteenth century testify to the lavish purchase of silk laces from Genoa for the trimming of costume. At the time of her death at the age of seventy, Queen Elizabeth is said to have possessed one thousand dresses. Many of these were diapered with gold and silver laces. Several were brought from Genoa and were inset with pearls and jewels. More than seventy years later Marie de Medici purchased *Point de Gênes* on a lavish scale. Towards the end of the seventeenth century this variety of lace was in general use in most of the European countries.

By a sumptuary law, the Genoese Republic forbade the wearing of gold and silver lace without the walls of the city. Both needlepoint and bobbin laces were important articles of trade, the latter known as *a piombini* being considered the more valuable. The Genoese workers specialized in the making of piece lace rather than lace by the yard. They specialized in making handkerchiefs, collars, aprons and fichus. Just as Venice was the centre for needlepoint lace in the sixteenth and seventeenth centuries, so was Genoa at that period the centre for the bobbin lace industry. The main seats of the industry were at Santa Margherita and Rapallo.

GENOESE 'COLLAR' LACE The cut-work or early lacis made in Genoa was altogether coarser than that of Venice. Nevertheless it was much in demand as a trimming for costume, particularly for out-of-door clothes. So extensively was it used for collars that Genoese lace was often referred to as collar lace. The custom arose of working the design of a grain of wheat into the lace as a symbol of Genoese workmanship.

MIXED LACE Genoese lace is usually classified as bobbin lace, but in reality it is a 'mixed' lace, being created of both needlepoint and bobbin laces. First, the design was traced on a pillow; later the mesh groundwork and fillings were added in needlepoint. Brides or tie-bars were usually adorned with picots. A special type of Genoese lace was evolved in the seventeenth century. This incorporated the use of a flat bobbin braid. It was termed Greek lace or *Point de Gênes grisé*. A woven braid was worked into a coarser and cheaper lace which was known as *Punto Mezzo*. The braid itself formed part of the design. It was puckered and shaped to conform with the lines desired.

Milan Lace

Milan lace is given precedence by many modern connoisseurs. There is a decided individuality in the laces made at this centre.

The lace-workers of Milan had achieved work of real merit in their *passements* into which they worked patterns of scrolls and flowers similar to those in the *Venetian Punto Tagliato à Fogliami*. The rich reliefs of the Venetian work were, however, lacking.

GUIPURE LACE Guipure lace became a speciality of Milan. Braid was used and the designs were rich with armorial bearings, crowns, eagles, flowers and scrolls. Later, in the nineteenth century, the Milanese confined themselves to making torchon laces.

Milan has the distinction of creating lace at a very early period. The earliest mention of Italian lace refers to Milan. A document dated 1493, sharing out property between two sisters, Angela and Hippolita Sforza Visconti, refers to Milanese lace.

English wardrobe accounts refer to this variety. Henry VIII was the proud possessor of an edging of lace made of purple silk and ornamented with gold and which had been brought from Milan. Anne of Denmark, the wife of King James I, possessed in 1606 'a suit with cannons thereunto of silver lace, shadowed with silk Milan lace'.

Other Laces of Italy

Bobbin lace was made on the island of Pelestrina in the nineteenth century. As at Burano in the same period, the industry represented relief measures in time of need. The lace made at Pelestrina was much in demand for household furnishings, for curtains and blinds, for counterpanes and chair trimmings.

Macrame lace was made in various centres in Italy, Milan being the chief. It was a popular variety in convents and was much used for the decoration of church furniture as well as for household trimmings. It was a knotted lace of Arabic origin.

BLONDE LACE At Albissola, near Savona, a black lace in imitation of that made at Chantilly was made. This industry rose to meet the current demand for blonde lace. Large quantities were exported to Spain. A special technique was required to make this lace, involving the use of huge cushions. Four or more women sat at one of these pillows manoeuvring sixty dozen or more bobbins. The Albissola workers made lace for the coronation of Napoleon.

Of interest rather than of importance was a fabric known as *Aloe lace*. It was made at several centres in Italy and was called *Fino d'Erbe Spada*. It was a coarse lace made from the fibres of the aloe. It was made either by tatting or by the twisting and plaiting of threads. Some threads were left natural-coloured; others were dyed black before being worked. The prosperity attached to this industry declined for the lace did not bear washing; it became mucilaginous.

The importance of the Italian lace-workers in both needlepoint and bobbin laces cannot be fully assessed. They provided the world market with lace during the greater part of the seventeenth century – a period when lace was used extensively. Not only did the lace-workers supply a current need but their work served as a foundation for the art of lace-making in other countries.

North Italy. Bobbin lace. Cuffs. Second half of the seventeenth century
UPPER: Length 9¼ inches. Greatest width 8¼ inches
LOWER: Length 15¼ inches. Greatest width 6½ inches

Italy. Milan. Bobbin lace panel à brides. *Seventeenth century*
The motifs show the influence of the art of the Near East

Brussels. Shawl of pillow-made lace. First half of the nineteenth century
The pattern is applied to a ground of machine-made bobbin net

French. Probably Binche. Bobbin lace. Cap crown and lappets

First half of the nineteenth century

CAP: $10\frac{1}{4}$ inches by $9\frac{1}{4}$ inches   LAPPET: 21 inches by $3\frac{1}{2}$ inches

THE LACES OF
THE LOW COUNTRIES

I N time sequence and in craftsmanship, the laces made in the Low Countries rivalled those of Italy with reference to both needlepoint and bobbin laces. It was in the latter type, however, that Flanders excelled.

CLOSE BOND BETWEEN ITALY AND FLANDERS It is significant that Italy and Flanders were European leaders in the industrial arts. It is noteworthy too that these two countries produced the finest pictorial art in the medieval and Renaissance period. These influences had far-reaching repercussions which had their bearing, among other things, on the making of fine lace.

There has been much discussion and dispute concerning the real originators of lace. Most authorities give preference to Italy in the matter of needlepoint lace but grant priority to Flanders in bobbin varieties. Whatever the truth, it must be borne in mind that a close bond united the two countries and there must have been inevitably a strong interplay of ideas and practices. The beauty and aesthetic charm of Italian art and craftsmanship proved an inspiration to the hard-working, artistic artisans of the Low Countries. In needlework, the close connexion between the two countries is evidenced by the pattern books of the late sixteenth century which were published simultaneously and which were very similar in character.

EARLY ILLUSTRATIONS OF FLEMISH LACE Portraits of the fifteenth century show that the people of Flanders delighted in wearing lace. The lace cornette or cap was much favoured. On an altar dated 1495, in the church of St Peter at Louvain, Quentin Mastys portrayed a girl making pillow lace with the aid of bobbins. It is thought that the occupation was an usual one at that period. Engravings by Martin de Vos, 1581, show a girl engaged in the same craft.

EULOGY OF A FLEMISH POET Writing verses in Latin in 1651, Jacob van Eyck, a Flemish poet, praised the lace-makers of his country:

'Of many arts, one surpasses all; the threads woven by the strange power of the hand, threads which the dropping spider would in vain attempt to imitate and which Pallas would confess she had never known.

'For the maiden, seated at her work, plies her fingers rapidly and flashes the smooth balls and thousand threads into the circle. Often she fastens with her hands the innumerable needles to bring out the various figures of the pattern, often, again, she unfastens them; and in her amusement makes as much profit as the man earns by the sweat of his brow; and no maiden ever complains at even of the length of the day.

'The issue is a fine web, open to the air with many an aperture, which feeds the pride of the whole globe; which encircles with its fine border, cloaks and tuckers, and shows grandly round the throats and hands of kings; and, what is more surprising, this web is of the lightness of a feather, which in its price is too heavy for our purses.

'Go, ye men, inflamed with the desire of the Golden Fleece, endure so many dangers by land, so many at sea, whilst the woman, remaining in her Brabantine home, prepares Phrygian fleeces by peaceful assiduity.' – *Urbium Belgicarum centuria.*

COMMERCIAL WORTH OF FLEMISH LACES Both needlepoint and bobbin laces became in the early sixteenth century articles of commerce. All Europeans coveted these fabrics and consequently lace was an important source of revenue to the Low Countries. For two centuries this commerce throve. The prosperity of the lace industry was accounted for, not only by the quality of the fabrics themselves, but by the patronage, encouragement and industrial liberty bestowed upon the lace-workers. The foundations of this prosperity were so firm that the industry remained secure at a time when every other industrial art was blighted by the severity and horrors of religious persecution.

This religious warfare in the Low Countries reacted to the good of the lace industries of surrounding countries. Many thousands of lace-makers settled in them with the result that the secrets of Flemish lace-craft were dispersed into every city of Northern Europe. The laces of the Low Countries are therefore noteworthy not only in themselves but because they form the source from which the lace-workers of many countries obtained their technique and designs.

When Colbert founded the lace manufactories of France, Flanders grew alarmed at the success which attended the efforts to lure her workers across the border. Colbert settled the foreign artisans in towns such as Aurillac, Sedan, Rheims, Le Quesnoy, Alençon, Arras and Loudun, where the townsfolk were already engaged in lace-making. At the expense of Louis XIV, the foreign lace-makers were engaged to teach all the processes of lace-making. According to Voltaire, thirty of these teachers came from Venice and two hundred from Flanders. This number was increased by mass migrations, and in 1698 an Act was passed by the Flemish government threatening dire punishment on all who should suborn Flemish craftsmen.

FLEMISH LACE SCHOOLS Lace-making was an integral part of female education in Flanders. At the age of five, a girl began her apprenticeship in an *école des dentelliers*; at the age of ten she earned sufficient to maintain herself. By that time she was able to manipulate the bobbins with wonderful dexterity.

These schools were much admired. There was a suggestion that similar schools should be set up in England. A tract published in London in 1577 and written by Andrew Yarranton, Gent., gives a graphic description of one of the Flemish lace-schools:

'Joining to this spinning school, is one for maids weaving bone lace; and in all towns there are schools according to the bigness and multitude of the children.

'I will show you how they are governed. First, there is a large room, and in the middle thereof a little box like a pulpit. Second, there are benches built around the room as they are in our play-houses. And in the box in the middle of the room, the grand mistress with a long white wand in her hand.

'If she observes any of them idle, she reaches them a tap, and if that will not do, she rings a bell, which by a little cord, is attached to the box. She points out the offender and she is taken into another room and chastised. And I believe this way of ordering the young women of Flanders is one great cause that they have so little twit twat and I am sure it will be well if it were so in England.'

The advent of the machine age did not mean the destruction of the lace-making industry of the country. Machine lace proved to be an abundant source of revenue, employing many thousands of the inhabitants. Belgium secured for herself a pre-eminent position and maintained this position despite the keen competition of France and of England. Brussels, Ghent, Alost and other centres had busy factories and derived handsome profits from machine-made nets and laces.

VARIETIES OF FLANDERS LACE Flanders lace is a comprehensive term and covers all those laces which were made in Flanders in the early period of development. It included among others, Flemish Point, Brussels Point, and much work that passed under the name of a misnomer, *Point d'Angleterre*. Gothic and Venetian styles were imitated in the earliest of the Flemish laces and then followed efforts to imitate the guipure laces of Genoa. The next progression was to *Point Gaze* which developed later into *Point de Bruxelles* and the modern appliqué.

The early laces were of a gossamer fineness. Design and *réseau* were worked flat; there was no cordonnet. Neither was there evident in any form that characteristic which was later to be a distinguishing feature of *Point d'Angleterre* and of Brussels lace, viz. the presence of loose threads on stems and leaves.

FLEMISH FLAX The lace-workers benefited by the close proximity of the much-coveted flax of Flanders. Thread made from this flax ensured that gossamer-like nature of the fabric which was so much sought after by the lace-workers and which they attained in so remarkable a degree.

SMUGGLING The story of lace has many facets. Among the most romantic are the stories of the smuggling of the treasured fabric. Much Flemish lace was smuggled into France by means of dogs. A dog was caressed and made a pet of in a French home; after a period of time it was taken across the frontier to a house where it was kept in a state of semi-starvation and ill-treated. Then the coat of a bigger dog was fastened securely to its body. This served to conceal a quantity of lace. The dog was set at liberty and encouraged to return to its French home.

That this smuggling by means of dogs was a common practice is evident from the statistics of the French Customs House. In the period 1820 to 1836 as many as 40,278 dogs were destroyed for smuggling lace and tobacco. The French government paid the reward of three francs for the capture of each of these dogs which were described as being of big size and capable of carrying as much as twenty-six pounds of contraband.

CLASSIFICATION OF FLEMISH LACES Eugene Van Overloop, in his authoritative guide to the laces of the Brussels Collection, lists the laces of Flanders under four general headings. Priority is given to the laces of Brussels and Brabant. Next are classified the laces of Flanders generally, then those of Mechlin and Antwerp; and finally the laces of Valenciennes and Binche. Technically the two main types, needlepoint and bobbin laces prevailed.

Bobbin laces were in three varieties. The lace-workers of Valenciennes, Mechlin, Binche and certain other areas in Flanders used the method known as *fil contenu*, wherein a continuous thread was worked upon a stationary pillow and so lace was formed. Much of the work was in *trolle Kant*. High relief was introduced by outlining the design in heavier thread.

Another technique involved the use of a movable pillow. By using a cushion of this type, the lace-worker could turn and adjust it in order to work the curves of the design with ease. The pattern was worked first and then many tie-bars or brides were added to form a mesh. A crochet hook was used to join the mesh and *toile*. This technique was favoured in particular in the making of the guipure laces of Brussels and of Bruges. It was known as *à pièces rapportées*.

Another variety of pillow lace was that known as *vrai réseau* or *droschel*, a type often referred to as hand-made bobbin net, a variety much favoured by the lace-makers of Brussels. The work was made in narrow strips which were joined together with the *point de raccroche*. The mesh of the one-inch strips which formed the lace was in itself a work of art and an achievement of which Brussels was justifiably proud.

The technique used by the Flemish needlepoint workers was the usual one of forming a framework of needle-stitching on parchment or paper bearing the design.

The lace-workers of the Low Countries at times combined needlepoint and bobbin laces. The usual procedure was to work the design on a pillow and add tie-bars to create a mesh in needlepoint. Lace of recent date made by this method was termed *Point d'Angleterre*, thus giving an additional connotation to a name already confused as to its meaning.

APPLIED LACE The popularity of Brussels appliqué bears witness to the prosperity of the applied lace industry in the Low Countries. The patterns were worked with a needle or with bobbins and were applied to a groundwork of machine-made net. Large pieces such as shawls and bridal veils were made by this method and were considerably cheaper than the hand-made specimens.

Another technique practised involved the embroidering of machine-made net. The design was embroidered in chain stitch or by stitches made with the aid of the crochet hook. This was called Tambour work or *tulle brodé*. When the design was embroidered with a needle it was sometimes called *broderie à l'aiguille*. The beauty of this work lay in the fillings of the designs. The fabric was inferior to *vrai réseau* for it was coarse and wiry, being made of cotton and not of the pure, superfine flax thread used in the making of *Vraie Angleterre* laces. The durability was lessened because of the practice of powdering the cotton fabric with white lead to bleach it.

Brussels Lace

Brussels enjoyed a favoured position in the Low Countries in that it was a court centre. The fine lace produced there, however, ensured for itself a pre-eminence by its own merits for the finest fabrics manufactured in the city rivalled those of Italy.

Lace was made in Brussels in the early fifteenth century, and elaborate specimens were presented to the churches by the princes of Brabant.

Point d'Angleterre was a name in common usage in the seventeenth century. When made in England by Flemish lace-workers it was inferior to the finest fabrics created in Flanders, for England could not produce the necessary flax which ensured lace fabrics of fine quality. Much of the choicest Brussels lace was smuggled into England and sold as English point. In 1678 the Marquis de Nesmond seized a vessel bound for England carrying as contraband a cargo of lace. Among the goods confiscated were 744,953 ells of lace and an incalculable number of collars, aprons, fichus, fans, gloves, handkerchiefs, all made of lace.

Writing in 1756, Mrs Calderwood in her *Journey Through Holland and Belgium*, described the lace-making industry of the time:

'A part of their work is grounding lace; the manufacture is very curious. One person works the flowers. They are all sold separate and you will see a very pretty sprig, for which the worker only gets six sous.

'The masters who have all these people employed give them the thread to make them; this they do according to pattern, and give them out to be grounded; after this, they give them to a third hand, who "hearts" all the flowers with the open-work. This is what makes the lace so much dearer than the Mechlin which is wrought all at once.'

SUPERIORITY OF BRUSSELS Brussels excelled above all other centres in the making of lace. Antwerp, Ghent, Binche and other towns emulated it but they did not succeed in creating fabrics of equal quality.

Much of the beauty of Brussels lace was due to the extraordinary fineness of the thread. Lace-workers who tried to copy the laces of Brussels despaired in their efforts for they could not hope to compete with the fineness of the thread.

SPINNING OF LACE THREAD Flax of a special kind was cultivated solely for the purpose of making thread for lace and cambric at St Nicholas, Tournai, Cambrai, Hal and Rebecq-Rognon. The thread made from it was of so fine a texture that it was liable to break and

4

as a preventative the flax of finest quality was spun in dark, damp, underground rooms, where only one shaft of light was allowed to penetrate. The spinner was content to *feel* rather than see the gossamer thread as it passed through her fingers. A panel of dark paper was fixed so as to throw the thread into relief. The spinner worked meticulously, examining in detail the thread drawn from her distaff.

The work demanded the greatest skill. Wages were proportionately high but they did not compensate for the conditions of work in a damp, unhealthy workroom. Brussels guarded closely the secrets of the spinning of this fine thread for she realized that it was this medium which contributed so largely to the high reputation of her laces.

NAPOLEON'S INTEREST IN BRUSSELS LACE Brussels lace was much favoured at the court of the first French Emperor. When Napoleon and Josephine made their first official entry into Brussels, the Empress received a gift in the form of a collection of the finest lace of the *vrai réseau* type. She also received an elaborate curtain made in Brussels point. It carried designs portraying cupids bearing cradles. These were supposed to be prophetic and emblematic of the birth of the King of Rome. Napoleon was well pleased with these gestures and gave in return orders for the manufacture of albs which were to be made in the most exquisite point for he intended them as a gift for the Pope.

After the Battle of Waterloo, a lace manufacturer of Brussels, M. Troyaux, converted his workshops into a hospital for forty English soldiers and provided them with all necessaries. His action, motivated by high and humane principles, brought him material reward. When he resumed business, so great was the demand from England and by British tourists for his lace fabrics that he soon retired, having amassed a great fortune.

PATTERNS OF BRUSSELS LACE The earliest patterns of Brussels lace are in the Gothic style. The motifs have precision and clear-cut lines. Gradually, the flowing lines showing Renaissance influence, were introduced into the designs. The outlines of scrolls, festoons and leaves were emphasized by a raised treatment. Among others, the English lace-workers of Devon became enamoured of these raised effects and they learnt the technique readily when Belgian teachers taught them. At the time when Brussels lace experienced its greatest demand in the period of the First Empire, designs included a multitude of flowers, sprigs, wreaths, columns and *petits semés*, including spots, stars and crosses. There was an Egyptian note in the introduction of palms and pyramids. These were discarded at the Restoration and flower designs prevailed once more.

GROUNDS OF BRUSSELS LACE Two grounds characterized Brussels lace. The bride was the earlier. This became very rare and expensive as time advanced. The other type was the *réseau* ground. This was made by hand, *à l'aiguille*, or on the pillow, *au fuseau*. The former was the superior kind and was worked in small sections, each strip being an inch wide. These strips were joined by a stitch much favoured by Brussels and Alençon lace-workers. It was called *Point de raccroc* or *assemblage* and it was known in England as fine joining.

The *réseau à l'aiguille* was seldom made after the invention of machine-made net. Grounds made *à l'aiguille* were three times as expensive as those made on pillows; but they were better for their wearing qualities and were not liable to ravel. The solidity of the needleground was ensured by the passing of the needle into each mesh for as many as four times. In the mesh of pillow lace this firmness was wholly lacking. The needleground had a further advantage in that it could be repaired quite easily and imperceptibly; pillow lace, when repaired, showed the joinings.

The motifs of Brussels lace were also of two kinds. Those made with the needle were called *à l'aiguille*, those on the pillow *point plat*. The latter were characterized by their yellow hue as they came from the hands of the lace-workers. To counteract this, the practice arose of placing the motifs in a small bag containing white lead and beating it with the hand. This had a dire effect on the health of the lace-workers and did not contribute to the preservation of the lace. When fabric treated in this manner was exposed to heat or to sea air, it invariably turned black and resisted all efforts at restoration.

SPECIALIZATION IN LACE-WORK So complicated were the methods employed in the making of Brussels lace that it was thought best to perfect the lace-worker in one of the highly specialized techniques and assign work to her in that particular process only. The *droscheleuse* made the *vrai réseau*, the *dentellière* the footing. The *fonneuse* made the open-work in the *plat* and the *jointeuse* united the different sections together. The *plat* flowers were made by the *platteuse*; the motifs were attached to the ground by the *appliqueuse*. As many as seven workers were required for a single specimen of Brussels lace.

POINT GAUZE A more modern variety of lace made in Brussels was, however, made by one worker only. She used the same thread throughout the fabric. This lace was known as *Point Gauze* or gauze point. The lace was needle-made, with a hexagonal mesh. The pattern and ground were made simultaneously. The fabric was made in small sections. These were joined together and the joinings were covered as in early point lace with leaves, sprigs and other motifs. The designs reflected Renaissance influences and effects of shading were produced by needle-darning.

Mechlin Lace

Mechlin lace was one of the prettiest of all lace fabrics and was termed by many the 'Queen of Laces'. It was made at Mechlin, Antwerp, Lierre and Turnhout. It was made in one piece on a pillow and, though called *Point de Malines*, it was not a point lace. Flowers were an essential part of the design. The lace was often called *Broderie de Malines* for the treatment of the flowers was reminiscent of that used in embroidery.

Up to the year 1665, Malines lace was a general term for all Flanders lace. The lace-workers of Bruges, Ypres, Dieppe and Courtrai were content to sell their work under that name.

A ban was placed by Charles II on all foreign laces and as a result but few pieces of Mechlin lace found their way into England at the period. When the ban was removed in 1699 Mechlin lace became one of the prime favourites and its popularity was maintained in eighteenth-century England.

MECHLIN LACE FAVOURED IN ENGLAND Press notices form some of the most fascinating of documentary evidence in the study of the history of lace. The *London Gazette* of August 17 to August 24, 1699, announced in its columns:

'Lost from Barker's coach, a deal box containing . . . a waistcoat and Holland shirt both laced with Mechlin lace.'

Before the repeal was established, Queen Mary bought, according to the Great Wardrobe Accounts, two yards of knotted fringe for her Mechlin ruffles. Mechlin lace was one of the favourites of Queen Anne. A memoranda of her expenses shows that on one occasion she bought eighty-three yards for £247.

During the Regency Period, Mechlin lace was much used in England. A favourite variety was that resembling the insertion of later centuries known as *campane*. It was light and fine and suitable for ornamenting gathered trimmings, for it had an edging on both sides. Mechlin lace was essentially an additional trimming. It did not in itself serve for the *grande toilette*. Yards upon yards of it were used for nightcaps, ruffles, cravats, lingerie; it was used yet more lavishly when Fashion decreed the use of India muslin.

AN EYE-WITNESS'S ACCOUNT OF THE MECHLIN LACE-WORKERS Writing of the town of Mechlin in 1756, Mrs Calderwood, an observant traveller, recorded:

'All the town is full of convents. Mechlin lace is all made there; I saw a great deal, very pretty and very cheap. They talk of giving up the trade, as the English, upon whom they depend, have taken to wearing the French blondes.

'The lace-workers employ the workers and all the town with lace. Though they gain but twopence-halfpenny daily, it is a good worker who will finish a Flemish yard (28 inches) in a fortnight.'

Napoleon's admiration for Mechlin lace accounted largely for the great demand for it under the First French Empire. An oft-related anecdote tells that when Napoleon first saw the exquisite tracery of the spire of Antwerp cathedral, he exclaimed, '*C'est comme de la dentelle de Malines*'.

CHARACTERISTICS OF MECHLIN LACE Mechlin lace was light and filmy, finer in texture than the finest Valenciennes. Its suppleness was treasured by those who applied it as an edging to muslin frills. It was easily recognized among other laces by a fine bright thread which outlined the designs.

Early Mechlin laces showed a number of varied grounds, the best known being the snow ground, *fond de neige*. Ultimately, after much experimenting, the lace-workers favoured a ground of small hexagonal meshes, reminiscent of the ground of pillow-made Brussels lace.

Designs varied with the time of production. At the height of its glory, the rococo style prevailed. Delicacy and transparency characterized the massed motifs. At the close of the eighteenth century, the lace-workers introduced into their fabric floral sprays and festoons which gave them a wide field for demonstrating their skill at making *jours* or fillings. When Napoleon was interested in this variety of lace, the patterns were not so concentrated. They were scattered as sprigs, blossoms and symbols over the fabric, an arrangement which showed in full effect the regularity of the meshes which formed the groundwork.

Antwerp Lace

Antwerp was an important centre of the lace industry. In the seventeenth century the city exported vast quantities of lace to the Spanish Indies. When the overseas market was lost, the lace-workers of Antwerp suffered severe hardships.

Lace continued as a local industry and supplied a home demand. Traditional designs were made, a favourite being the *potten Kant*, or pot lace. The flower-pot was symbolical of the Annunciation. In early illustrations of the visit of the Angel Gabriel to the Virgin Mary, the flower-pot was shown. It was usually filled with lilies. With the decline of Roman Catholic fervour, the vase alone remained. Embroiderers had favoured it as a design and lace-workers introduced it into their fabric. The flower-pot varied in shape and size and also in its position on the lace. Large flowers were also prominent in the designs of Antwerp lace. These were held together by brides.

EARLY PATTERN BOOK   What is accredited as being one of the earliest pattern books was published at Antwerp. It was printed by Vosterman and was illustrated by six wood-cuts. These showed six women and one man making lace on frames. The title was in English:

'A neawe treatys; as cocernynge the excellency of the nedle worcke spannishe stitche and weavynge in the frame, very necessary to al theym wiche desyre the perfect knowledge of seamstry, quiltinge, and brodry worke, coteinynge an cxxxviij figures or tables, so playnli made and set tout in portraiture, the whiche is difficyll; and natolye for crafts me but also for gentleweme and ioge damosels that therein may obtayne greater conynge, delete and pleasure.

'These bokes be to sell at Andwarp in the golden Unycorne at Willm Vorstermans.'

Ghent

THE INTEREST OF THE BÉGUINES IN LACE-WORK   Many travellers passing through Ghent on the 'Grand Tour' in the eighteenth century wrote accounts which testify to the flourishing lace industry of the city. The chief lace work was done by members of the religious sisterhood, the Béguines in the lace schools attached to the béguinages.

The industry continued to flourish down to the close of the nineteenth century but the demand for the laces of Ghent was somewhat reduced. A valuable letter, 'Answer to Sir John Sinclair', written in 1815 by Mr Hey Schoulthem, portrays the lace industry of the time. The writer explained that at the time of the French invasion of the Low Countries, the lace trade of Ghent was flourishing. Men and women were engaged in making lace. Holland, France and England were the main commercial markets. Many of the laces made in charitable institutions were exported to Spain and her colonies.

PROSPERITY IN THE MACHINE AGE Ghent had no reason to lament the invention of machine-made fabrics. The fame of Ghent as a centre of the lace industry was not eclipsed. The city turned its attention to the making of machine net and laces. The net made at Ghent was a very fine variety which served as an excellent foundation for elaborate embroidered work. Limerick lace, as it was made in the earliest period of that industry, was copied very closely; in fact, the similarity was so close that differentiation between the two was often difficult even to the eyes of the initiated. The lace workers of Ghent also made great quantities of hand-made imitations of Valenciennes lace when an earnest demand for these types was made.

Holland

The rich lace fabrics of the Flemings overshadowed the laces of the Dutch. Nevertheless, lace of lasting worth was made in Holland. Much of this supplied a ready market in France.

When large numbers of refugees settled in Holland following on the Revocation of the Edict of Nantes, they were welcomed heartily. Lace-workers were among the artisans who settled in the country. At the Orphan House at Amsterdam, a factory was established for making a special kind of point lace known as *dentelle à la Reine*. It was mainly due to a Huguenot named Simon Chatelain that the industry of gold and silver lace-making was introduced into Holland.

No foreign laces were imported into the country but the Dutch exported laces to Italy. In 1770 Maria Theresa crippled the expansion of the lace trade of Holland by issuing a declaration prohibiting the importation of Dutch lace into any of her hereditary dominions in Germany.

A treasured possession preserved in The Hague is the shirt worn by William the Silent when he was assassinated in 1584. The linen shirt is decorated with lace in linen thread. The shirt had been described as thick, durable, strong and serviceable, characteristic of the wearer and of the people whom he formed into the Dutch Republic.

DECORATING OF HOUSES WITH LACE A quaint custom observed in Holland was the decorating of household ornaments with lace. A traveller in France wrote in 1691: 'The warming-pans and brasses are not here muffled up in much point and cut-work after the manner of Holland.' Another Dutch custom was to tie up the door-knockers with rich Dutch point lace to announce the birth of a child.

CHARACTERISTICS OF DUTCH LACE   The Dutch excelled in the making of bobbin lace. Much of this was used to ornament the national head-dresses. The lace had a marked solidity and closeness which necessitated a close examination of the fabric in order to fully appreciate the beauty of the design. So close was the texture of the lace that it resembled early cut-work on fine linen.

The motifs favoured were those of fruit and flowers represented naturalistically. A very usual motif was a conventional oval shape believed to have evolved from a representation of a chrysanthemum. Oriental flowers were depicted in Dutch designs following on trade with the East. *Potten Kant*, the symbolical flower-pot, was another usual motif. It was often shown between two confronted birds.

Mechlin. Bobbin lace. Part of a flounce. First half of the eighteenth century
Length: 4 feet 9 inches   Greatest depth: 24 inches

Brussels. Pillow-made lace. Portion of an apron
First half of the eighteenth century

Flanders. Antwerp. Bobbin lace. Three borders. Eighteenth century

'*Potten Kant*'. Top: length, 19 inches; width, 4 inches.　　Middle: length, 20 inches; width, $4\frac{1}{4}$ inches.
Bottom: length, $19\frac{3}{4}$ inches; width, $5\frac{7}{8}$ inches

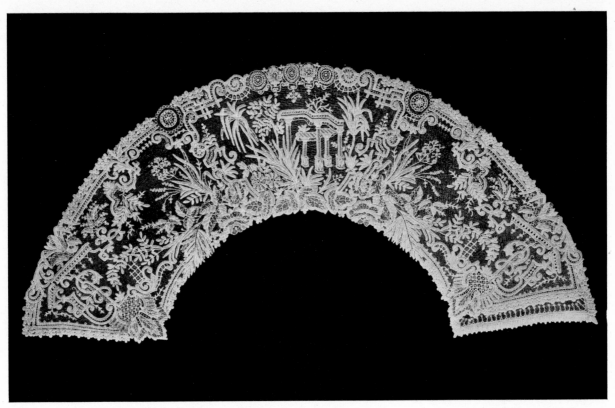

Brussels. Point de Gaze. *Fan mount. Needlepoint lace. Mid-nineteenth century*

Width: $20\frac{1}{4}$ inches   Depth: $5\frac{7}{8}$ inches

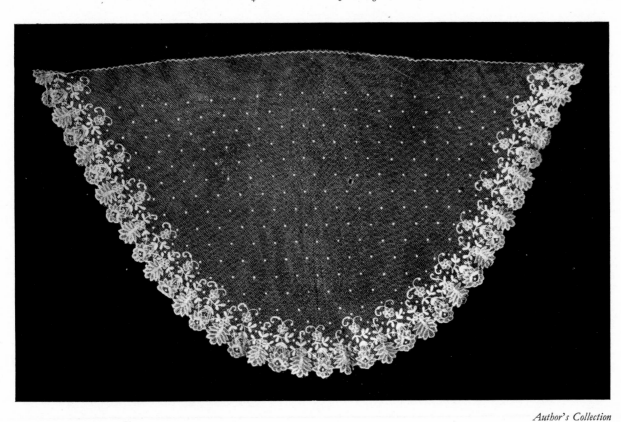

Brussels. Christening veil. Early nineteenth century

Width: 22 inches   Greatest depth: 18 inches

Machine-made mesh with *fond de neige* or snow ground.
Bobbin-made appliqué'd motifs inspired by Mechlin designs

Brussels. Wedding veil. Early nineteenth century

Length: 4 yards 15 inches. Greatest depth: 40 inches

Machine-made net.   Bobbin-made appliqué'd motifs showing the rose in several forms

THE LACES OF FRANCE

RANCE showed at an early period an active interest in the making of lace. The interest of the French court in this fine fabric gave a definite fillip to the industry within the country itself and indirectly it had repercussions on the lace industries of other European countries.

ITALIAN INFLUENCE In early Renaissance years, France was obliged to import her laces from Italy and the Low Countries. In the sixteenth century, Italian influence was strong owing to fashion's demand for *points coupés* and lace. Under the Valois and Medicis, the vogue for these was rivalled by that for embroidery and gold and silver lace. In the years of growing national consciousness, France grew averse to the practice of importing laces. As time advanced, French financiers decried the policy of buying foreign laces as it was a drain on the national revenue. France began to encourage Italian and Flemish workers to settle within her realm.

LACE CENTRE AT LE PUY A flourishing lace centre existed in France in the sixteenth century. This was at Le Puy. Lace at this period represented a transition from white embroideries to lace. It had closer affinity with embroidery and cut or drawn thread-work than with lace in the modern interpretation.

SUMPTUARY EDICTS The efforts of the lace-workers of Le Puy to establish a sound industry seemed doomed to disaster when the Seneschal of Le Puy passed sumptuary laws imposing a heavy fine on those who trimmed their clothes with lace. His economic insight was blurred by his desire to maintain social distinctions. His real purpose in issuing the edicts was to maintain the standards between high and low and he feared derogatory results if all classes were allowed to wear lace. As a result of this legislation, the lace-workers were faced with dire poverty. An edict of Louis XIII passed in 1629 allowed for 'a consumption of lace provided they were manufactured in the kingdom at a cost not exceeding three livres the ell for insertion and edging'. The Parliament of Toulouse issued through the Seneschal of Le Puy a severer edict. It forbade under payment of a heavy fine 'everybody of either sex, quality or condition from wearing any sort of lace, whether of silk or white thread with glittering passement of gold or silver, real or false'.

ST FRANÇOIS REGIS A Jesuit Father visited the lace-workers in their distress and distributed material relief and spiritual advice. He was deeply moved by the suffering around him and said: 'Have confidence; pray God to help me and lace-making shall not perish.'

He journeyed to Toulouse and interceded with the Parliament on behalf of the Auvergnese lace-workers, and through his efforts the decree was revoked. He helped the lace-workers by enlisting the help and protection of the Spanish Jesuits who assisted them when they travelled across the Pyrenees to sell their fabrics. Prosperity and wealth returned to the lace-makers of Le Puy. They honoured the Jesuit Father as a patron saint of lace-making and the Roman Church canonized him as St François Regis.

CATHERINE DE MEDICI The Italian-born queen of Henry II of France, Catherine de Medici (1519-1589), is popularly accredited with the distinction of having laid the main foundations of the lace industry of France prior to Colbert. She took a practical interest in the lace schools and set a fashion for the use of lace. It is recorded that 'the girls and servants of her household consumed much time in making squares of *rezeuil*'. Her bed was draped with squares of *rezeuil* or *lacis*. An inventory of Catherine's possessions at her death showed that she possessed a coffer holding three hundred and eighty-one of such squares ready for mounting. In another coffer were five hundred and thirty-eight similar squares bearing designs of flowers, rosettes and nosegays.

About the year 1585, Queen Catherine persuaded with great bribes a Venetian designer named Vinciolo to settle in France. He was to make ruffs and gadrooned collars. The Queen had set a fashion for the Medici collar and she gave the Venetian the monopoly for selling ruffs and collars of this type.

VINCIOLO'S PATTERN BOOK Vinciolo collected a number of patterns suitable for ruffs. Under the patronage of a later Queen of France, Louise de Vaudemont, wife of Henry III, he published a pattern book which bore the date 1587. The title of this book was 'The singular and new designs and work for linen for use as patterns for all sorts of stitches and cut-works, lacis and others. Dedicated to the Queen. Newly invented to the profit and content of noble ladies and young ladies and other gentle spirits, *amateurs* of such art.'

He used the word *amateur* in its original sence of lover and derided the published works of his predecessors. In his preface he stated: 'Si les premiers ouvrages que vous avez vus ont engendré quelque fruit et utilité je m'assure que les miens en produiront davantage.'

For twenty years new editions of this work appeared, each one containing new designs. In his verbose style, Vinciolo declaimed in the preface: 'I have greatly desired to place before you, for works of a magnificent standard, the present designs, which I have kept back hidden and unknown until now, when I offer them with a cheerful heart to the French nation.' It may be that he deluded himself to some considerable degree on the extent of his originality. He safeguarded himself by owning that he had 'obtained from Italy certain rare and singular patterns and having originated a few to the best of my poor powers'. He was careful, however, to claim for himself full credit for his efforts. 'I think, friend and reader, that you will not ignore in any way the great and sedulous labour I must have expended in drawing and giving light to the larger quantity of most excellent patterns for needlework contained in this present book.'

OTHER PATTERN BOOKS Vinciolo's book was used in many countries, but it is just to reflect on the pattern books which appeared in France before his publication. Francisque Pelegrin published a pattern book in Paris in the reign of Francis I. Six pattern books were published at Lyons. Two were dated 1549 and 1585. One of the undated books contained an elaborate design showing St Margaret holding a cross and defying a dragon. A pattern book published in Paris contained an interesting feature in the form of a ballade of twenty-eight lines written as a song for lace-makers.

VENETIAN INFLUENCE IN FRANCE Catherine de Medici deepened Italian influence in France. Although the influence of the city was declining, Venice was still the prime centre of fashion and luxury. The raised points of Venice were still coveted as were also her laces of gold and silver thread which were used as trimmings for cloaks, mantles, hats and boots. Queen Catherine encouraged vast expenditure on dress hoping that splendour of apparel and of equipment would blind the French nation to the poverty of its political condition.

At this stage, the lace made in France was a close replica of that made in Italy. It remained for the grand age of Louis XIV to nurture, to a glorious florescence, laces that rivalled closely those made in Venice but which were characterized by a beauty which was wholly French.

SUMPTUARY LAWS REGULATING THE USE OF LACE Sumptuary edicts were passed by the French government restricting the extravagant use of lace. Ten were proclaimed during the last half of the sixteenth century, but it is apparent that they were not enforced strictly. The nobles followed the royal example and adorned themselves with vast quantities of gold lace. When further edicts were passed in the opening years of the seventeenth century, Henry IV made obeisance to austerity and wore a 'doublet of taffety without trimming or lace'. Sully may have been responsible for this trend in fashion, for he waged war incessantly on the importation of lace. 'It is necessary', he said, 'to rid ourselves of our neighbours' goods which deluge the country.' No French subject was to transact with a foreign lace merchant save under pain of corporal punishment.

THE MEDICI RUFF Under the Medicis, the ruff was a special object of fashion interest. Henry II had favoured it to conceal a scar, and the fashion continued to prevail in the reigns of his sons. At first the ruff was of a simple type but later it was gadrooned and trimmed with geometric patterns of needlepoint and cut-work. The influence of the Flemish and Dutch painters penetrated into lace designs.

The ruffs worn in the French court grew to a tremendous size and became objects of derision for the caricaturists of the time. Pierre de l'Estoille in his *Journal de Henri III*, wrote: 'Ces beaux mignons portoient . . . leurs fraizes de chemise de toute d'atour empesez et longnes d'un demi-pied, de façon qu'à voir leurs testes dessurs leurs fraizes, il sembloit que ce fut le chef de Saint Jean dans un plat.' The journalist spoke truly when he said that a man's head complete with ruff resembled the head of John the Baptist on a charger. So cumbersome were the ruffs that the wearers could not eat in comfort. It is recorded that Reine Margot was obliged to eat her soup with a spoon which had a handle two feet long because she wore a ruff which was a monstrosity.

THE FALLING BAND   In the reign of Henry IV and his successor, Louis XIII, the pleated ruffs were replaced by wide flat collars made of Dutch linen. These corresponded to the 'falling band' of the English Stuart court. Men wore these collars trimmed with wide laces which fell down below their shoulders. Women wore these collars raised fan-fashion behind their heads. Portraits of Marie de Medici show that she adopted this fashion. Sharp indentations were now replaced by smoothly scalloped edges. Geometric motifs gave way to floral designs. Expanding tulips were popular as units in these patterns.

EXTRAVAGANT USE OF LACE   The use of lace in France was now greater than ever before. It was used to trim male and female costume. Inventories refer to lace-trimmed great collars, coats, cuffs, gloves, breeches, doublets and boots. Furniture was swathed in lace. Beds had head- and foot-boards trimmed with this fabric. There were lace canopies and lace-trimmed pillars supporting them. An inventory relating to the effects of Charles de Bourbon, 1613, and that of his wife, Countess of Soissons, refers to a bed decked 'with a pavilion of linen hangings, with bands of net made up of squares, the head-board covered with similar material, the inside of the canopy, the covers for the pillars, three curtains and a head curtain, a sheet of similar linen with a band of *rezeuil*, a state coverlet, all bordered with lace'.

Windows were trimmed with lace. Not only the windows of houses were decorated in this way but those of the great coaches and carriages that travelled along the new high-roads.

PICTORIAL RECORDS OF CURRENT FASHIONS   Engravings of the time record faith-fully the use of lace. Quicherat, in his *Histoire de Costume en France*, declared: 'There is hardly a specimen of Abraham Bosse's work which does not display the forms of collars, frills or cuffs' worn at the time. In his picture entitled 'The Prodigal Son', he portrayed the mother welcoming home her repentant son and encouraging his faltering footsteps onward by holding out to him a collar decorated with fine needlepoint lace. His picture of Dives showed him sitting at a table adorned with lace, and that of the Foolish Virgins showed them weeping into lace-trimmed handkerchiefs. Another of his pictures showed the 'Interior of a Lace Shop in the Galerie du Palais'. When Louis XIII, with religious severity, banned the use of lace, Abraham Bosse made a series of caricatures purporting to relate to the effects of the law. One picture was entitled 'Courtier Obeying the Last Edict', and showed a dandy of the time hurling his lace-trimmed costume on to a chair and dressing himself in a severe habit. His valet stood near, ready to lock away the beautiful clothes. A companion picture was that entitled 'A Lady of Fashion Discarding her Laces', and showed a lady placing elaborate laces in a coffer.

The edicts must have been accepted with deep regret, for France was deeply enamoured at this period with *Point de Venise*. All other varieties of lace had fallen into disfavour and France in general voiced the opinion of Seguin, a devotee of Venetian point. 'If perfection can exist on earth, it has been attained by the makers of lace and this specially applies to the Venetian lace of this period.'

HENRY OF NAVARRE FOSTERS INDUSTRY IN FRANCE   Henry IV realized that the use of lace had been carried to an excess. Anxious to foster home industry and craftsmanship, he established the Royal Tapestry Manufactory in 1607. In 1598 he caused to be planted in the Bois de Boulogne fifteen thousand mulberry trees in order to foster the silk industry. Sully, his austere Huguenot minister, showed himself intolerant of the King's enterprise. He said to his sovereign: 'You want iron and soldiers and not laces and silks to trick out fops.'

IGNORING OF THE 'CODE MICHAUD'   Edicts continued to be proclaimed in succession against the extravagances of the nobles. When Louis XIII married Anne of Austria, Italian laces were discarded in favour of Spanish laces, and royal personages showed an ill example of the austerity which they urged on the populace. The most celebrated of the proclamations issued was that known as the *Code Michaud* which classified and exorcised details of dress. It was greeted with derision and never came into effect. Satirists and caricaturists found in these edicts fertile ground. 'Le Courtisan Réformé, suivant l'Édit de l'année 1633' showed a young nobleman dressed in a plain costume looking disconsolately at a box of prohibited laces.

> Il me semble pourtant à mes yeux
> Qu'avec de l'or et la dentelle
> Je m'ajuste encore bien mieux.

An indication of the extravagance of the nobility in possessing lace fabrics is apparent from the fact that Cinq Mars, one of the leading nobles of the court of Louis XIII, left at his death three hundred sets of collars and cuffs trimmed with lace.

At the end of the reign of Louis XIII there existed centres of the lace-making industry as distinct from those of embroidery. The reign of Louis XIV extending over sixty-eight years witnessed the development and apogee of French needlepoint.

The regency of Anne of Austria was a period of many sumptuary edicts, for the taste for fine lace had become grotesque. Boot tops, for instance, were voluminous, and the space between leather and limbs was filled with expensive lace ruffles. Mazarin was interested in fostering the new lace industry of France. When besieging a town he was engaged in buying laces from Italy and Flanders. These were intended as patterns for Point de France.

A sumptuary edict prohibiting the use of foreign laces was passed in 1660 on the eve of the marriage of Louis XIV. Gala dresses trimmed with guipures, Genoa Points and *Points Coupés* had been bought in readiness. The edict decreed strict regulations concerning the wearing of French laces. Collars and cuffs of lace were given a year's grace and after that they were not to be worn at all. They were to be replaced by linen collars which might be trimmed with lace of one inch in width and of French manufacture.

The edict was received with bitterness for the French people had prepared in readiness for the royal wedding. Sganarelle, in Molière's *École des Maris*, commented on this edict:

> Oh! trois et quatre fois béni soit cet édit,
> Par qui des vêtements de luxe est interdit!
> Les peines des maris ne seront plus si grandes,
> Et les femmes auront un frein à leurs demandes.
> Oh! que je sais au roi bon gré de ses décris!
> Et que, pour le repos de ces mêmes maris,
> Je voudrais bien qu'on fît de la coquetterie
> Comme de la guipure et de la broderie!

The ordinance of 1660 was not observed strictly. Others followed prohibiting in particular points of Venice and Genoa.

SATIRIC VERSES IN ANSWER TO SUMPTUARY EDICTS In answer to the edict of 1660 a group of fashionable ladies meeting at the Hôtel de Rambouillet wrote, in 1661, the celebrated *Révolte des Passements*. This set of satirical verses has been treasured through the centuries because of its technical interest, for every lace of established importance at that period was mentioned, together with details of its characteristics and beauty.

The various laces are represented as meeting together, united by a fear that, after the recent enactment, lace as a luxury of dress was doomed to extinction. They agree to revolt and assemble in battle dress. Each vies with the other in courageous speech but all run away when opposed. *Une grande Cravate* rallies them and calls over a muster roll of *Escadrons de Niège*, *Dentelles de Moresse*, *Dentelles de Havre*, *Points d'Espagne*, *Escrues*, etc. At the approach of artillery, all surrender and are condemned. The points are to be made into tinder for the use of the King's Mousquetaires and the laces are to be converted into paper. Passements, Gueuses and silk laces are to be made into cordage and sent to the galleys. The gold and silver laces are to be burnt alive. Through the intercession of Love, '*le petit dieu plein de finesse*' the laces are pardoned and restored to court favour. The literary worth of the verses was topical and transitory; but, to collectors of lace, they have been of incalculable worth as determining the names, dates and relative values of the laces of the seventeenth century.

When Louis XIV married the Spanish Infanta, Spanish lace, and in especial black lace, came into favour. It was worn with gowns and with doublets of gold and silver brocade. For a period the gold and silver points of Spain and Aurillac rivalled the thread needlepoint of Italy and Flanders.

Royal edicts encouraging the French to wear the coarser laces of their own country having failed, the French government was now faced with the expediency of establishing other means of consolidating within the country the vast sums dispersed annually by the wearers of lace.

COLBERT'S ACTIVE INTEREST IN THE LACE INDUSTRY OF FRANCE   Colbert, Louis xiv's minister of finance, determined to develop the lace industry of France to such a degree that it could produce fabrics which could rival those produced in Italy and Flanders. He employed some of the best lace-workers of these countries and established them as teachers in French centres where a tradition of lace-making already existed. Pupils, already familiar with needle or bobbins, proved apt. Among these early centres were Sedan, Rheims, Le Quesnoy, Alençon, Aurillac, Arras and Loudun.

ALENÇON   Colbert set up a lace factory at Lonray, near Alençon, and appointed as manager Madame Gilbert. Under her were thirty forewomen who had come from Venice. The work made at this centre pleased the King who declared it to be superior to the needlepoint of Venice. The fabric came to be known as *Point de France*. In 1665 the manufacture was founded on royal ordinance and the decree stated 'that there shall be established at Guesney, Arras, Rheims, Sedan, Château-Thierry, Loudun, Alençon, Aurillac, etc., manufactures of all kinds of works with thread, either with needle or upon pillow, like those made in Venice, Genoa, Ragusa, and they will be called Points de France'.

ARGENTAN AND THE CHÂTEAU DE MADRID   Encouraged by the success of Lonray, Colbert set up another lace factory at Argentan, and at the Château de Madrid in the Bois de Boulogne. This latter specialized in work for the royal household, and the patterns for the fabric made here were designed by the foremost artists of the time.

THE LACE FACTORIES PROSPER   These factories proved lucrative and Colbert is reputed to have said to Louis xiv: 'There will always be fools enough to purchase the manufactures of France, though France should be prohibited from purchasing those of other countries.' Louis rewarded Colbert for his efforts in fostering home industries by making him chief director of trade and manufactures in the kingdom, a position which he filled with zeal. There was a remarkable increase in the number of lace-workers and the lace industry of France flourished.

The laces now made in France had definite local characteristics. They had emerged from the collective type known as *Point de France* and were far removed from *Point de Venise* which they had at first copied. Soon the laces of France supplanted the Italian laces they had once rivalled. The price of French lace made it somewhat prohibitive but the demand for it continued to increase. Little wonder, therefore, that Colbert observed: 'Fashion is to France what the mines of Peru were to Spain.'

COLBERT'S PROTECTIVE POLICY   During the infant stages of the lace industry France pursued a protective policy, ensuring the healthy growth of her enterprise. All foreign laces were forbidden. A special decree forbade 'the production, sale or use of any kind of thread point laces made with the needle, whether old or modern, except those made in the Royal manufactures'.

THE RETALIATION OF VENICE Venice realized that her lace industry was doomed if more and more of her lace-workers were lured away to France. Other artisans such as glass- and mirror-makers had been bribed into employment by Louis XIV. The Venetian Republic issued a decree declaring the emigration of artisans into France a state crime:

'If any artist or craftsman practises his art in any foreign land, to the detriment of the Republic, orders to his return will be sent him; if he disobeys them his nearest of kin will be put into prison in order that through his interest in their welfare his obedience may be compelled. If he comes back, his past offence will be condoned and employment for him will be found in Venice; but if, notwithstanding the imprisonment of his nearest of kin, he obstinately decides to continue living abroad, an emissary will be commissioned to kill him, and his next of kin will only be liberated at his death.'

In the face of these dire threats, France allowed the Venetian women to return to their homes. They had done their work admirably and the French women had proved themselves clever pupils. Voltaire recorded that in a short space of time sixteen hundred girls were in full-time employment at the royal centres of the lace industry.

Technique and design in early *Point de France* was of a high standard. The fabric created was light and the outlines of the pattern emphasized by overcasting over horsehair.

Flat *rabats*, or falling collars, were still favoured by men. Cuffs of fine lace were also worn. Prelates favoured fine guipure laces. Guipure laces were also used by women for their *berthes* or sleeves. When sleeves were short the laces were called *engageants;* when long, they were called *pagodes. Volantes* or flounces of lace were worn on skirts. These were trimmed with *tournantes* or *quilles* and were attached to dresses by *engrêlures* or footings. *Barbes* and *fontanges* of lace served as head-dresses. Handkerchiefs, fichus and scarves were all trimmed with lace.

Louis XIV was surrounded by clever artists. These he employed not only at the tapestry studios at Gobelins but at the lace manufactories. Artists like Le Brun and Berain introduced artistic patterns into lace fabrics.

Point de France held a supreme position in Europe. Watteau's painting entitled 'The Presentation of the Grand Dauphin to his Royal Father in 1668' shows the child wrapped in a mantle of the richest point. By royal command *Point de France* was used to trim the sheets of Holland linen used at the ceremony of his nomination. Louis XIV presented as a wedding gift to Mlle de Blois, toilet hangings 'garnie de point de France si haut qu'on ne voyait point de toile'.

FRENCH BOBBIN LACE Bobbin lace was rated less highly than needlepoint, but the former variety received an impetus from the demand for point lace in the seventeenth century. Those who could not afford needlepoint and who wished to rank among the fashionable wearers of lace contented themselves with the cheaper bobbin laces.

Lace was worn by men and women on every possible occasion. The artists of the seventeenth century depicted it at every opportunity. The paintings and portraits of Van Dyke, Rubens and Rembrandt, the engravings of Abraham Bosse, the interior scenes of Fragonard and Watteau record the fashions of the time.

THE STEINKIRK Officers of the army wore lace on their uniforms. The fashion of wearing a 'Steinkirk', or lace scarf, is said to have originated on the battlefield. At the battle of Steinkirk in 1692 the officers were suddenly called into action. They had no time to fasten their lace cravats in the elaborate methods practised at that time. They knotted these scarves simply and drew the ends through a buttonhole. For the next fifty years the men and women of France and England followed this custom.

THE ORIGIN OF THE 'FONTANGE' A chance incident is also said to have originated the fashion of wearing a high head-dress known as a *fontange*. At the time of its greatest popularity, the *fontange* was made up of tiers upon tiers of point lace borne on wires. It had begun, however, as a low covering which was artistic and graceful. When La Fontange, a favourite of Louis XIV, was out hunting, her hair became disarranged from the ribbons which bound it. Hurriedly, she bound her hair with a lace handkerchief. The king was so charmed with the coiffure that he ordered her to adopt it for a court function, and so a new fashion was created.

PUPPETS DRESSED IN LACE The custom of dressing up puppets in lace, fashionable at the time, was developed in the reign of the Grand Monarch. Dolls were used much after the fashion of modern illustrated magazines to show the prevailing fashions. The puppets were made of wood and cardboard. The face was usually made of wax. The most famous doll of the reign of Louis XIV was called *La Grande Pandore*. It was exhibited in the latest court dress. A smaller doll was called *La Petite Pandore* and was shown in the Hôtel Rambouillet, dressed in clothing suitable for morning wear.

Dolls such as these were sent off to Italy, Vienna, England and other countries, for Paris fashions were eagerly sought after. These puppets were exposed for public view at fairs. This practice became established in the eighteenth century. So important was the regard for these *poupées* in England, that when the British ports were closed to the ships of France in war-time, the dolls, *Grands Courriers de la Mode*, were granted entry into the country by special permission. These dolls were draped in the finest of French laces. A record of 1764 stated: 'There has been disembarked at Dover a great number of dolls, lifesize, dressed in the Paris fashions in order that the ladies of quality can regulate their taste on the models.'

THE REVOCATION OF THE EDICT OF NANTES The Revocation of the Edict of Nantes was an ordinance of incalculable importance in the history of lace. It meant disaster to the French lace industry; it brought inspiration and wealth to that of neighbouring countries. Those capitals of Europe where religious toleration prevailed received vast contingents of French citizens, the majority being the most skilled and most worthy in the country.

PROTESTANT ARTISANS In the early years of Louis XIV, Protestants were, in the main, in charge of the factories of France. Roman Catholic dogma of the time looked askance at usury and at many of the financial methods accepted in business enterprises; and so the Huguenots, hampered by no such opinions, found in the manufactories a free field of endeavour.

RELIGIOUS PERSECUTION OF THE HUGUENOTS 1685 Trouble befell them when the Edict of Nantes, granting religious liberty, was revoked in 1685, and Louis XIV, influenced by Mme de Maintenon and the Jesuit Confessor, La Chaise, entered upon a rigorous policy of religious persecution, believing this policy to be essential for the well-being of the Roman Catholic Church. Persecutions and forfeitures drove thousands upon thousands of industrious Huguenots to Flanders, Germany, England and Switzerland. They were dependent on their skill. They set up factories and manufactured fabrics which France found herself compelled to buy.

France herself was reduced to creating only the coarser laces which she had formerly despised. Colbert saw the downfall of his schemes. There is an element of pathos in his leter to M. de St André, the French ambassador in Venice. He asks him to supply detailed information concerning the laces of Venice and Burano. 'Let me know if they are made in such large quantities as in former times and where they are exported.' He ends the missive with the observation that the main trade in *Point de Venise* had returned to its birthplace.

EXTRAVAGANT FASHIONS UNDER LOUIS XV The use of lace finery increased under Louis XV. It was an important accessory in the toilette of every man and woman of fashion. The ceremonies and stately etiquette of the royal court prescribed the use of lace.

When a lady was presented in a royal drawing-room, she was decked in the finest point laces. A court robe or train eight ells in length trailed after her. Plumes were fastened to her hair. Point lace lappets hung from her head according to the regulation length prescribed by the respective degrees of nobility. Princesses of the royal blood wore full-length lappets.

The accounts of Mme Dubarry show her prolific use of *Point d'Argentan* and *Point d'Angleterre*.

LACE USED FOR INTERIOR DECORATION The age of Louis XV was an age of elegant dishabille. Toilet tables, curtains, bed-coverings, pillow-cases were all trimmed with costly lace.

The Marquise de Créquy related how her aunt, the Dowager Duchesse de la Ferté, had a quilt made of one single piece of Venetian point. 'I am certain', she wrote, 'that the trimmings of her curtains, which were of *Point d'Argentan*, were worth at least forty thousand écus.'

The artist Bonnard portrayed the interior of a dressing-room and showed it as furnished with fine laces. On either side of a Venetian mirror a pair of guipure lace curtains were draped. The toilet table had a cover trimmed with a deep flounce of needlepoint. The lady wore a dressing-gown made of guipure lace; a wide flounce of *Point de France* was attached to the bottom and the sleeves were edged also with a rich variety of *Point de France*. A deep flounce of *Point de France* was draped at the back of the wash-stand.

THE MORNING RECEPTION French sophistication in the eighteenth century expressed itself in unconventional receptions. Women of fashion invited their friends, both male and female, to a *ruelle*, a morning reception where the hostess reclined on a bed. Vallances, coverlets, counterpanes, pillow-cases were trimmed with fine lace. England imitated France in this custom. The *Royal Magazine* of 1763 reported that on the occasion of the baptism of the Duke of York, the state ministers went to the council chamber at St James's where a splendid bed was set up for the Queen to sit on. The counterpane was of fine workmanship and the lace trimming it was worth £ 3,783 sterling.

In *A Wreath of Fashion*, the English poet Tickell described the duties of a critic at a *ruelle*.

> Oft with varied art, his thoughts digress
> On deeper themes – the documents of dress;
> With nice discernments, to each style of face
> Adapt a ribbon, or suggest a lace;
> O'er Granby's cap bid loftier feathers float
> And add new bows to Devon's petticoat.

The *réveillé* became the most fashionable reception. Costly lace was in great demand. The bed furnishings of the Queen of France were renewed every year and the discarded laces became the perquisites of the royal mistresses.

THE BATHROOM RECEPTION French receptions were held not only in the bedroom but in the bathroom. The hostess reclined in a bath up to her chin in water which was *au lait*, i. e. clouded with perfumes and essences. A broad flounce of point lace was attached to the bath. Towels and bath mat were trimmed with costly point, as was also the lady's *peignoir*.

Lace was used in enormous quantities for fan leaves and the artistic lace fan reached an excellence in the reign of Louis xv which was never afterwards equalled. Antique sticks were used of ivory, gold, silver, wood, tortoise-shell and lacquer. These were set with precious stones, and hand-carved metals. Appliqué lace was used for fan leaves. Black, white and cream motifs were applied to chiffon. Lace was sometimes used in conjunction with paintings.

Lace was used to trim all manner of accessories and the people of the time were fortunate in having so wide and excellent a range to choose form. Rothomago in *Le Palais des Dentelles* writes:

> Je demandai de la dentelle:
> Voici le tulle de Bruxelles,
> La Blonde, le point d'Alençon,
> Et la Maline, si légère;
> > L'application d'Angleterre
> > (Qui se fait à Paris, dit on);
> > Voici la guipure indigène,
> > Et voici la Valenciennes,
> Le Point d'esprit, et le point de Paris;
> > Bref les dentelles
> > Les plus nouvelles
> Que produisent tous les pays.

PRE-REVOLUTION FASHIONS Under Louis XVI there was a marked taste for laces of great lightness. The book of the dressmaker of Marie Antoinette, that of Mme Eloffe, gives ample evidence for the Queen's predilection for blonde laces. The Queen set a fashion in pseudo-simplicity but the costumes of men continued to be elaborate and were trimmed with jabots and fichus of great price. A man of fashion required vast quantities of these before he considered his equipment complete. The Archbishop of Cambrai possessed forty-eight pairs of ruffles of Mechlin, *Point de France* and Valenciennes; the latter lace was usually reserved for evening wear. Louis XVI possessed, in the year before his death, fifty-nine pairs of new lace ruffles; ten of *Point d'Angleterre*, twenty-one of Valenciennes and twenty-eight of point.

The period of the French Revolution was disastrous to the lace industry of France. The traditions of an art which had once been the glory of the nation was completely lost in many areas.

REVIVAL OF INTEREST IN LACE UNDER NAPOLEON Napoleon was attracted by the industry of lace-workers and determined to foster the industry at Alençon. He revived the court etiquette of Louis XIV and required the wearing of point lace at state functions. Imperial orders for lace included a bed-trimming of lace costing 40,000 francs. It had a powdering of bee devices. The escutcheons of Marie Louise were added when the coverlet was transferred to her from the Empress Josephine. The Emperor ordered for his second wife, as marriage gifts, bed furnishings comprising curtains, coverlets, vallences and pillow-cases trimmed with Alençon lace. *Point d'Alençon* was also chosen as a trimming for the layette of Napoleon's little son. Thus there came a brilliant, if transient, period of prosperity to the lace industry of France. The lace-workers abandoned the old points and concentrated on the flowing lines of Renaissance designs. An attractive feature was their rose points in double and triple relief.

Needlepoint fabrics were supplanted by embroidered Indian work, by drawn muslin and blonde laces. Inventories and trousseaux bear witness to the enormous use of these fabrics. In the court reaction against the extravagance of pre-Revolution days, the simplicity of muslin was enthusiastically received. Lace was used to trim the embroidered fichus and scarves worn.

MACHINE-MADE LACE In 1818 bobbin net machines of France began to produce quantities of net and tulle. Calais, St Quentin, Douai, Cambrai, Rouen and Caen became seats of the tulle manufacture. Silk net was made at Lyons Lace ornaments made on the pillow and in needlepoint were applied to the machine-made fabrics, but the makers of hand-made lace had received a fatal blow. The prices of hand-made lace were lowered to compete with the machine-made varieties but with little effect. The hand-workers found a more secure market in exporting their work to America.

Thread lace suffered disastrously with the introduction of machine-made net but the silk lace industry received a favourable impetus. The blonde laces of Chantilly and Bayeux became very popular, for the brilliancy of the silk ground was something which a mere machine could not achieve. These fabrics declined in popularity later when silk net lace was invented.

Interest in 'old lace' waned. The prime factor was cheapness, for it was necessary to compete with machine-made goods. Cotton thread was manufactured about the year 1833. Lace-workers decried its lack of artistic merit but welcomed it as a medium of their craft, for it was pliable and less liable to break.

Hand-made lace is still favoured in France. Very little, however, is manufactured in the old lace centres. In certain provinces in the Haute Loire, the Puy de Dome and Brittany, for example, the craft is still preserved, and lace-workers delight in making guipures and blondes in cotton, in silk and in wool.

The Needlepoint Laces of France

Point de France

This was a general name given to the needlepoint of France prior to the time when it became distinguished by local names.

Under Louis XIV, the grounds of this needlepoint had regular meshes which were large and decorated with tiny picots or loops. The mesh was reduced in size and the *petit réseau*, or ground of small meshes, evolved. The picots were then dispensed with and the regularity of the mesh was left clearly in view.

Designs were magnificent and copied closely those of Venetian points. Floral devices sprung from bold scrolls. The bigger blossoms were accentuated in parts by raised stitching. Designs degenerated to the pretentious rococo style. Towards the later years of the long reign of the Grand Monarch, fantastic figures and attributes were introduced into the pattern. The Sun King himself was portrayed and also men and women in contemporary costume. Pseudo-Oriental designs were introduced and these were copied by contemporary lace-workers in Flanders and in Italy with a diligence which later centuries have decried as unfortunate.

Alençon Lace

In the early years, following on Colbert's patronage of the lace industry, the lace-workers clung as closely as they could to the traditions of the Venetian school. From about 1678, however, Alençon point began to show individual characteristics, and from that date it ceased to be called *Point de France* and was known as *Point d'Alençon*.

EARLY PROSPERITY ATTENDS THE ALENÇON INDUSTRY Mme Despierres, in her *Histoire du Point d'Alençon*, has shown that the lace-workers of Alençon showed great talent and earned high wages from the commencement of royal interest. Her examinations of wills and marriage contracts have produced conclusive evidence of the diligence of the workers and of their financial gains. A family named Barbot was amongst the most successful. The mother saved 500 livres; her daughter Marthe on her marriage contributed 300 livres towards her dowry, the money representing her own savings. Another daughter, Suzanne, had as her wedding portion '6,000 livres earned in making cutworks and needlepoint which commanded a high price'.

Under the patronage of Louis XIV and Colbert, the technique of the lace-workers at Alençon continued to advance, and lace of a very fine texture was produced. *Point d'Alençon* was termed a winter lace as the fabric was firm; this was largely due to the strong cordonnet. Outstanding delicacy of workmanship called for designs which were clear and well-defined, and the leading artists of the day contributed their patterns. A preference was shown for a clear ground which threw into relief the elegance of the design. The fabric was executed in the finest flax which was obtained from Flanders.

THE ALENÇON CORDONNET The cordonnet of Alençon lace was a distinct characteristic. It differed from that of other French laces in that it had a foundation of horsehair. This was inserted also into the tiny loops or picots, inserted in the spaces between the scrolls and flowers.

There is record of a collar made at Venice for Louis XIV. The lace-workers were unable to find horsehair sufficiently fine, so they inserted their own hair instead in order to obtain the fine delicacy of work which they sought. This collar cost the Grand Monarch 250 golden *écus*.

The Alençon lace-workers buttonholed closely in the finest thread over the horsehair placed along the outline of the design. A firm cordonnet enhanced a lace but in the use of horsehair lay the seeds of decay. When the lace was washed, the horsehair contracted. The mesh and the design puckered and the whole fabric deteriorated. Late Alençon workers took the precaution of removing the horsehair padding.

ALENÇON GROUNDS The earliest laces made at Alençon had grounds in which the mesh was large and hexagonal. Buttonholing was close and even. Later a fine, small hexagonal mesh was evolved. The workers dispensed with picots, for they had no reason to cover up the regularity of the mesh. They advanced from *bride bouclée*, or buttonholing, to *bride tortillée* in which a twisted thread was used. The groundwork was made, not after the usual manner in a large piece, but in strips measuring an inch in length; these were linked with fine joining.

AN EXPENSIVE FABRIC Throughout the long reign of Louis XIV, Alençon point lace flourished and prospered. The demand for it continued unabated in the reign of Louis XV and extravagant prices were paid for it. The high price was justified by the workmanship. An intricate and elaborate flounce required as many as eighteen workers for a single section of the lace.

After the eclipse of the Alençon industry at the time of the Revolution, it revived through the interest of Napoleon. But much of the past traditions of the Alençon centre were lost and it was only with real difficulty that lace-workers could be found to execute the imperial orders. Alençon point as an industry became virtually extinct with the downfall of the first French Empire.

Point d'Argentan

A fine needlepoint lace was made at Argentan. It is very probable that the factory was established by Colbert in the reign of Louis xiv, although there is no real documentary evidence to prove this.

Point d'Argentan and *Point d'Alençon* were the only two needlepoint laces made in France bearing a net ground. There existed a strong resemblance between the two varieties and they were often confused. These two laces were often used in combination with a particularly harmonious result.

The Argentan workers employed at an early stage *bride tortillée*. They twisted a whipped thread around each of the six *brides* which formed a single mesh.

Improvements in the meshes of lace led to an impoverishment of design and the lace-makers endeavoured, when this became perceptible, to make good the loss by introducing fanciful *jours* or *modes* into the centres of blossoms or into spaces in the patterns. A fashion followed of introducing these fillings over a wider field and they were found in the borders of laces, in medallions and shells and in the spaces between garlands.

The lace-workers of Argentan employed larger and bolder patterns than those of Alençon. The *réseau* was coarser and the *toile* flatter.

The Argentan workers excelled above all others in making *brides*, or bars. A special feature of their lace was the *bride picotée*, a legacy from the early Venetian instructors. These *brides* were formed of hexagonal buttonhole bars. They were fringed with rows of purls on each side. Such a bar was known as *bride épinglée*, as pins were pricked on the pattern to show where the loops, or *bouclés*, were to be made.

When the lace-workers were driven into exile by the Revocation of the Edict of Nantes, the lace industry of Argentan suffered severely. A demand for the fabric continued, however, during the reigns of Louis xv and Louis xvi; but it became almost extinct with the Revolution.

Much of the beauty of Argentan needlepoint can be attributed to the exquisite designs created by such masterly artists as Le Brun, Bailly and other skilled draughtsmen.

Bobbin Lace

EARLY PEASANT LACES Long before Colbert established a prosperous lace industry in France simple bobbin laces, finely wrought, were being produced. Technique and patterns had a definite *locale*. The laces were much sought after for ornamenting the traditional and elaborate peasant head-dresses. Although these laces never achieved prominence commercially, they were, nevertheless, of real artistic merit. Generally speaking, they were made in scattered homes throughout the country, but some lace centres existed. Among these was that at Caen, where lace resembling that of Chantilly was made. Le Havre, Le Puy, Dieppe, Bayeux were other flourishing centres. Lace was made of sufficient merit and was made in sufficient quantities to allow for export to other countries. Lace of a high standard was made by the peasant women of Normandy. Their style of work resembled closely that made by the lace-workers of Flanders.

Valenciennes Lace

By a treaty of 1678, dividing up the province of Hainault, Valenciennes ceased being Flemish and was transferred to the jurisdiction of France. Bobbin lace had been manufactured at this centre since the fifteenth century, having been introduced there by Pierre Chauvin.

Valenciennes lace took pride of place among Flemish lace for fineness of fabric and beauty of design. The centre of the manufacture in the time of Louis XIV was Le Quesnoy.

CHARACTERISTICS OF VALENCIENNES LACE After much experimenting, the laceworkers of Valenciennes favoured a ground which was later to form a characteristic feature of the lace. The mesh was square or diamond-shaped, of great regularity and very open. Each side of the mesh was made up of four closely-plaited threads. The ground and the floral ornament were worked simultaneously with thread of the same quality. Unlike Mechlin lace there was no outlining thread to emphasize the design. The absence of such a thread conduced to easy laundering, a characteristic which made 'Val' lace eminently suitable as a trimming for articles requiring frequent washing.

USES OF THIS VARIETY OF LACE The nobility of the eighteenth century chose Valenciennes lace to trim their elegant dishabilles. The lace-workers pandered to fashion and created filmy fabrics with light flower patterns set off by a groundwork of meshes which formed a trellis ground for the whole. French influence showed itself in an orientation away from the Flemish patterns with their large scrolls which had featured in early Valenciennes work. Valenciennes lace experienced a greater reputation when it appeared with designs showing light and graceful clusters and detached sprays resembling those used in *Point d'Alençon*.

'VRAIE' AND 'FAUSSE' LACES Valenciennes lace was divided into two types – *vraie* and *fausse*, the connotation referring to lace made within the town and that made in the neighbourhood.

M. Dieudonne, Préfet in 1804, stated in his *Statistique du Département du Nord*:

'This beautiful manufacture is so inherent in the place, that it is an established fact, if a piece of lace were begun at Valenciennes and finished outside the walls, the part which

France. Chantilly fan. Circa 1850–70

Width: 24 inches. Greatest depth: 7¼ inches

The mount of the fan is made of bobbin lace. The guards and sticks are of tortoise-shell

France. Needlepoint lace. Point de France. End of the seventeenth century
Length: 33¾ inches. Depth: 13¼ inches

France. Point d'Argentan. Flounce. Circa 1700
Length: 8 feet 9½ inches. Greatest depth: 31 inches

Victoria and Albert Museum

France. Lille. Veil. Mid-nineteenth century

had not been made at Valenciennes would be visibly less beautiful and less perfect than the other, though continued by the same lace-maker with the same thread and upon the same pillow.'

The townsfolk maintained that this difference was due to the change in atmosphere. The lace was made by young girls working in dark underground cellars where the moist atmosphere prevented breakages in the thread. As a result of being confined for many years in the darkness, many of the lace-workers became blind by the time they reached the age of thirty.

Workers of *Vraie Valenciennes* could not make more than an inch and a half a day. '*All made by the same hand*' was a proud boast entered on the bills of the lace-workers.

Referring to Valenciennes lace in 1788, Arthur Young wrote: 'Laces of 30 to 40 lines' breadth for gentlemen's ruffles is from 160 to 216 livres (£9 9s) an ell. The quantity for a lady's head-dress from 1,000 to 24,000 livres. The women gain from 20 to 30 sous a day. 3,600 persons are employed at Valenciennes and are an object of 450,000 livres, of which the flax is not worth more than 1/30. The thread costs from 24 to 700 livres the pound.'

CENTRES OF THE INDUSTRY OUTSIDE VALENCIENNES   Up to the period of the French Revolution, the town of Valenciennes and its neighbourhood had been the centre of this particular industry. Later the industry was carried into two provinces of Belgium. The lace was made in convents and béguinages. Ypres made a fine quality of Valenciennes lace. Other centres were Poperinghe, Courtrai and Ghent.

Chantilly Lace

THE DUCHESS DE ROHAN   Chantilly lace-workers were producing lace of merit in the sixteenth century. The lace of this area achieved renown in the mid-seventeenth century following on the interest of Catherine de Rohan, Duchesse of Longueville, member of an ancient Breton family distinguished for its leadership of the Huguenot cause. She established a lace school at her château in Étripagny. Here lace-workers from Chantilly, Le Havre, Dieppe and centres in the Île de France rallied and experimented and achieved the creation of the double or Chantilly ground.

The early laces had no outstanding artistic merit. *Gueuse* and *Point de Paris* were made but these were regarded as inferior to Mechlin and Valenciennes. Chantilly sprang into fame by making silk laces, and in especial laces of black silk.

A feature of old Chantilly silk lace, whether of white or black, was the pattern of a vase or flower basket. This motif was used also on Chantilly pottery which enjoyed a reputation as high as that of Chantilly lace.

In the manufacture of their black laces, the workers of Chantilly used a silk called *grenadine d'Alais*. By the twisting of the threads, the lustre of the silk was concealed and the finished lace looked as though it had been made of flax. The mesh created was called *fonds chant*, the name being a play on the word Chantilly. The fillings entered into the design had special names according to the place where they were made and were called *cinq trous*, *vitré*, or marriage.

Black silk lace was used extensively for outdoor costume. Members of the aristocracy and of the upper bourgeoisie invested in the purchase of black silk lace. Chantilly black lace shawls and scarves and fans were handed down the generations as precious heirlooms.

At the time of the French Revolution many of the lace-workers of Chantilly died at the scaffold, and it seemed that the industry would become extinct, but prosperity returned about 1805 when white silk lace became fashionable. There followed a revived demand for black silk lace. Large amounts were made for the home market and for export to America.

In this revival the lace-workers of Normandy, and in especial those of Caen and Bayeux participated. The making of lace became a valuable subsidiary industry in areas devoted to agriculture.

ENGLISH INTEREST IN CHANTILLY LACE The black silk lace made at Chantilly and in Normandy found a sure market in England. In the Victorian era there was a fashion for black silk shawls. These were worn folded in half, the points reaching down to the hem of the long skirt. By the folding of the front of the shawl, the wearer displayed her elegance and the shawl or brooch pin which secured the garment in place was a symbol of her taste and financial worth.

Lille Lace

Lace made at Lille and at Arras resembled that made at Mechlin. In the seventeenth century, the bobbin lace-workers of Lille made their fabric from hempen thread which was spun at Châlet-sur-Moselle. The lace was of the guipure variety and was classified as a *passement*. In the second half of the seventeenth century efforts were made to create a delicate fabric. A Mignonette lace with double ground was made.

FEATURES OF LILLE LACE The groundwork of Lille lace was clear and large. Two threads were twisted together on each of the four sides of the mesh. Simple patterns were favoured. No cordonnet was used; but the outlines of the design were emphasized by the application of a loosely-spun flax thread of a glossy nature. The older varieties of Lille lace had straight edges which ran vertically and horizontally, irrespective of the curves of the pattern.

Black silk lace was manufactured at Lille in the eighteenth century, but the interest was only transient and the lace-workers returned to the making of white lace. Tiny square dots which featured in old Lille lace were retained in later specimens, and designs favoured by the lace-workers of Mechlin were copied.

Lorraine Laces

The laces of Lorraine are sometimes classified as Saint Michael laces, for that town was the main centre of their manufacture. The laces made in the area resembled those of Lille. A pattern called *Point de Flandre* was very usual. Application flowers were made and attached to the *réseau*. A happy feature of these sprigs was their white quality as they came from the hands of the workers; there was no necessity to bleach them with white lead or any other injurious material.

The lace made in Luneville, Dijon, Lyons, Auxerre, St Étienne, the Île de France, Sedan and Rheims found good markets in Britain, America and the East Indies.

Mirecourt Lace

Le Puy and the neighbourhood entered on the manufacture of lace on a considerable scale in the seventeenth century. The lace-workers began modestly and aimed at imitating the laces made at Lille; but later they surpassed their models. Brussels lace was copied in the nineteenth century and sprigs and flowers were imitated with remarkable exactitude. When machine-made grounds were available, hand-made flowers and sprigs were applied on to them after the manner of Honiton lace.

Arras Lace

Arras was, from the earliest times, renowned for its tapestries and needlework. It became famous for its bobbin lace which was identical with that made at Lille. The Flemish character of the designs is explained by the fact that until the Treaties of Aix-la-Chapelle (1668) and Nimeguen (1678), Arras and Lille belonged to the Netherlands.

The Emperor Charles V is reputed to have first introduced the lace industry to Arras. The industry flourished until the close of the eighteenth century. In 1788 Arthur Young wrote, 'coarse thread laces, which find a good market in England, are made in Arras. The lace-workers earn from 12 to 15 sous per day'. There was an immense demand for Arras lace during the period of the First French Empire (1804–1812).

Arras lace never reached the standard of Lille lace. Early work was done in coarse thread; this gave place to finer thread. A pattern known as *Mignonette* was a prime favourite. The range of patterns was small but this resulted in greater dexterity, and the lace-workers of Arras worked with astonishing rapidity. Stiffness characterized the patterns and the edges of the lace were straight, not scalloped. The lace was durable, firm and perfectly white.

For a period the lace-workers of Arras specialized in the making of gold laces. Britain bought immense supplies of Arras lace, including gold lace. Three hundred and fifty-four yards were bought to trim the coronation robes of George I.

Blonde Laces

USE OF FLOSS SILK Blonde laces were so called because they were, at first, made from a filmy Chinese floss silk which was blonde or *natural*-coloured. Later the silk was dyed in different colours, but some of the most attractive specimens were made in the blonde floss. Later two different sizes of thread were used in its manufacture; a fine thread was used for the mesh ground and a coarse, fluffy thread for the design.

SILVER 'BLONDE' As progress was made in the art of bleaching, silver-coloured floss was produced and laces in this fabric were in much demand. The next progression was the creation of black blonde laces.

Spanish patronage led to increased production of black blonde lace. The mesh was large and open and of a cobweb fineness and was much favoured as a material for mantillas. Designs reflected Spanish influence. Big, flowery motifs were made in close stitchery and of a satin sheen. These were in vigorous contrast to the delicate net groundwork.

DECLINE OF BLONDE LACE The vogue for blonde lace passed, though a passing revival was achieved for it by the Empress Eugénie. The blonde lace manufactured at Caen was decorated with fine pearls and was much sought after. Chantilly, Bayeux, Dieppe were other centres of this variety of lace.

Hand-made lace fought a losing battle against machine-made lace. Though the latter lacked artistry and elegance, ultimately it prevailed. Chantilly workers made black lace in the first decade of the twentieth century, albeit on a limited scale.

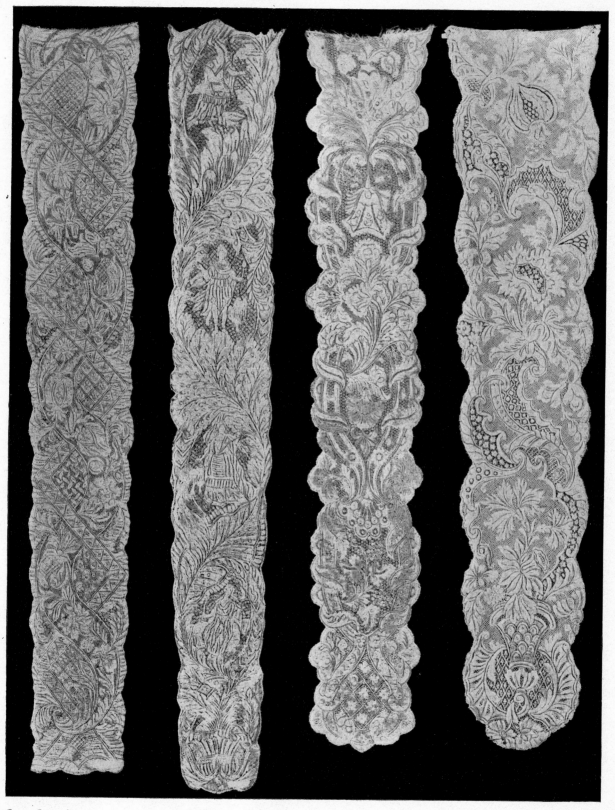

France. Valenciennes. Bobbin lace. Four lappets or barbes
First and second decades of the eighteenth century. Approx. length: 24 inches.   Width: 4 inches
Round Mesh. Calle Maillé Ronde   TECHNIQUE: *Fil contenu*

France. Probably from Caen. Veil. Bobbin-made silk blonde. Circa mid-nineteenth century

Size: 50 inches by 55 inches

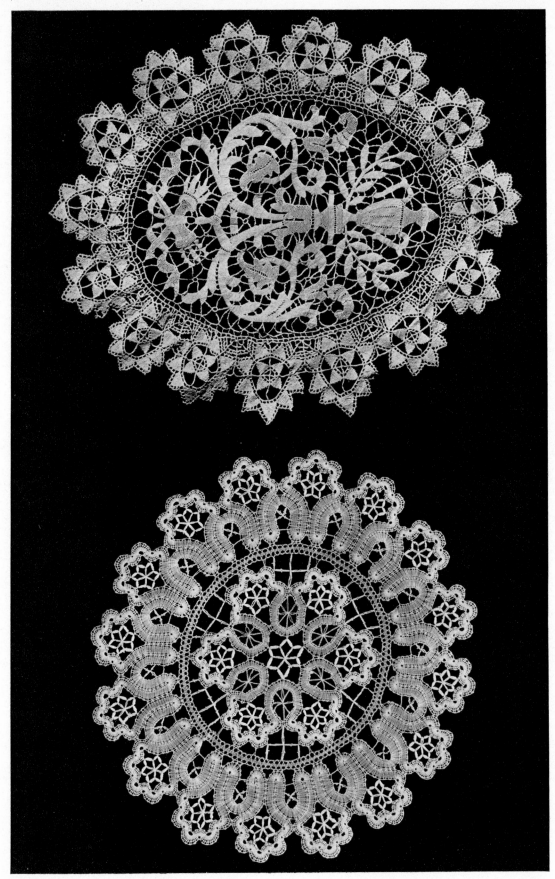

ABOVE: *Cyprus lace. Needlepoint. Nineteenth century*
The design consists of a vase with floral sprays within an oval shape.
Star-shaped motifs form the border

BELOW: *Czechoslovakian lace. Bobbin-made mat. Nineteenth century*

Size: 14½ inches diameter

ABOVE: *Maltese lace. Flounce of pillow-made lace in cream-coloured silk*

Victoria and Albert Museum

Early nineteenth century. Length: 10 feet $\frac{3}{4}$ inch. Depth: 2 feet $6\frac{1}{2}$ inches
The Maltese Cross is introduced into one set of designs and also along one edge

BELOW: *Greek lace. Zante. Edging. Needlepoint. 1630.*

The Needlework Development Scheme, Glasgow

Size: 12 inches by 5 inches

THE LACES OF
OTHER EUROPEAN COUNTRIES

Spain

SPANISH POINT experienced for a period a reputation as renowned as that of Flanders and Italy.

Some authorities hold that Spain learnt the art of making needlepoint from Italy and that it was the lace-workers of the Spanish peninsula who communicated the knowledge to the Spanish dependency, Flanders. It is also maintained that the Flemish lace-workers in gratitude taught the art of pillow lace to the Spaniards. Another theory is that the Spanish learnt lace-craft from the Moors.

Whatever the origin, Spanish point was much valued. Its manufacture was widespread within the peninsula and the standard of the work was such that Spain disdained the fine needlepoints of Venice and Genoa.

EXCLUSIVENESS OF SPANISH LACE The reputation of Spanish point was to remain insular for a long time. This was due to prescribed policy. Dress as worn in the Spanish court was governed not by the decrees of fashion but by the sumptuary laws of the country. These were of a negative nature and gave very little encouragement to the advertisement of lace fabric outside the Spanish Empire. The demand for Spanish lace was so high at home that there was never sufficient to meet requirements.

LACE FOR CHURCH USE Spain was pre-eminently Roman Catholic in outlook and lace fabrics were needed not only for court dress and for high festivals but to deck the incalculable number of images of Our Lady. These were dressed and redressed daily in innumerable churches. Lace was also needed for altar cloths, for albs and for general church purposes. The laces, worn by the more favoured of the Madonnas, were of such high value that ladies of the royal blood were appointed by the Church to be mistresses of the robes. These offices were much coveted. When Spain had any lace left for export, it was reserved for her rich gold colonies.

Point d'Espagne in its generic sense referred to gold and silver lace. This was sometimes embroidered in colours.

The early pattern books contained designs for working in gold and silver thread, a commodity monopolized in many parts of Europe by Jewish families. Thread lace had been in use in the fifteenth century. One of the greatest treasures of the cathedral at Granada is an alb presented by Ferdinand and Isabella. It is symbolic of the work created for the splendour of Holy Church.

The fine church lace of Spain was hidden from the eyes of the world until the time of the dissolution of the Spanish monasteries, when they became dispersed abroad. The specimens included not only heavy Spanish point but pieces of astonishing fineness made evidently not from commercial motives. They were offerings of pious devotion.

THE VISIT OF PRINCE CHARLES OF ENGLAND In 1623 Philip III issued an ordinance for simplicity of dress. The law was suspended for the matrimonial visit of Prince Charles – later King Charles II of England. On his arrival at Madrid, the Prince received from the Queen of Spain ten trunks of richly-laced linen. Charles had travelled incognito and was represented as being ill-provided. In reality, the young gallant had been well-equipped. The Great Wardrobe Accounts enter under the heading of *Extraordinary Expenses of His Highness to Spain* 1623, the following items:

14 Ruffs and 14 pairs of cuffs laced, at *20s* . . . . £14; For lacing 8 hats for the footmen with silver parchment lace . . . . £1 4*s*.

SPANISH FASHIONS IN THE SEVENTEENTH CENTURY The fashions prevalent among the ladies of Spain in the seventeenth century are described in *The Letters of a Lady*, published in London in 1679:

'Under the vertingale of black taffety, they wear a dozen or more petticoats, one finer than the other, of rich stuffs trimmed with lace of gold and silver, to the girdle. They wear at all times a garment called sabenqua; it is made of the finest English lace and four ells in compass. I have seen some worth five or six hundred crowns . . . so great is their vanity, they would rather have one of these lace sabenquas than a dozen coarse ones; and either lie in bed till it is washed or else dress themselves without any, which they frequently enough do.'

The writer gives an account of her visit to the Princess Monteleon:

'Her bed was of gold and green damask, lined with silver brocade and trimmed with *Point d'Espagne*. Her sheets were laced round with an English lace half an ell deep. The young Princess bade her maids bring in her wedding clothes. They brought in thirty silver baskets, so heavy, four women could only carry one basket; the linen and the lace were not inferior to the rest.'

Much of the English needlepoint lace used in Spain was purchased by way of the Low Countries.

Point d'Espagne reached its highest reputation at the time of the marriage of Louis XIV of France and the Spanish Princess. There exist elaborate descriptions of the celebrated gold bed at Versailles and of the furnishings of the royal carriages, and there are inventories of velvet and brocade coats and dress, all these being adorned with *Point d'Espagne*. Spain herself became attracted by French laces and many were imported from the neighbourhood of the Île de France.

VARIETIES OF SPANISH LACE Gold *Point d'Espagne* was in greatest demand. An old Inquisition banner preserved at Valladolid had a border of *Point d'Espagne* and carried a geometric design. Gold lace featured largely on the mantles of priests and grandees when they processed at religious fêtes.

Silver *Point d'Espagne* was used on court dress. It was worn on the uniform of a noble order of chivalry, the Maestranza.

Spanish needlepoint was worked much more closely than its Italian counterpart. Outstanding among the many excellent Spanish needlepoint laces of the sixteenth century, is that which was known as *Punto in Espana frisado en oro*. It was appealing in texture, in design and in colouring. A gold thread, fashioned into small picots, was used to outline the motifs. The gold thread was also introduced into the centre of the design. Around it was stitchery and weaving of polychrome silk. During the seventeenth century, the lace-workers introduced a symbol into their work as a mark of identification. This was a combination of a branch of a tree, which was made to lie diagonally, and a curved leaf.

The many Spanish portraits of the seventeenth century testify eloquently to the lavish use of lace. Considerable quantities of Italian bobbin lace were imported into Spain to decorate the enormous ruffs which were worn at that period. The best lace-work of Flanders also entered Spain and served for use and inspiration.

One of the most renowned of Spanish laces was that known as *Point de Milan*. The name refers to the lace and has no localized bearing to the city of that name. Upon a groundwork composed of an open square mesh were massed motifs; these included geometrical forms, elaborate scrolls and blossoms and the national emblem of Spain, the pomegranate.

When the lace industry was fostered by the state in France, Colbert saw commercial possibilities in *Point d'Espagne*. It was supposed to have been introduced into the country by a French Huguenot named Simon Chatelain, who received protection for his advanced religious views in return for his services to the lace industry. These prospered and France soon exported *Point d'Espagne* to Spain.

SPANISH BLONDE LACE Blonde lace was made in Catalonia. It did not fully satisfy the tastes of the Spanish duennas who preferred to import their blonde laces from France. Much of the blonde lace made in Spain was exported to America. The work was done on a domestic basis by women and children. There were no established factories as in France. National symbols were worked upon the laces; Spanish castles, well-turreted, were surrounded by the eagles and lions of the royal house of Castile and also by masses of archaic figures and stylistic birds.

Blonde laces were required for the national head-dress, the mantilla. The olive-skinned ladies of Spain decked themselves in white blonde lace on state occasions.

Mantillas were also made from deep flounces of black blonde lace. The *mantilla de tiro* for ordinary wear was usually of black silk and velvet. These head-dresses were treasured greatly. They were sacred by Spanish law and could not be claimed as a payment for debt.

Dentelles de Moresse were also made in Spain. These laces are often referred to as 'morisco work'. The lace was of a chequered variety and the patterns were of peculiar interest. They did not resemble those current in Europe and owed their origin to Moorish influences. As in other forms of Moorish art, no living creatures were represented as Mohammedan law proscribed their inclusion.

Portugal

Portugal was interested primarily in needlepoint. As in Spain, the work was carried on by individuals. There were no established manufactories such as existed in France.

Lisbon was celebrated in the eighteenth century for a coarse white bobbin lace. Madeira lace made in the Torchon variety was also renowned. Much of this lace-work was done entirely by men. Women concentrated on the famous Madeira embroidery. Patterns of these coarse laces were mainly Greek and Maltese in origin.

A sumptuary law of 1749 prohibited the wearing of lace. After the Lisbon earthquake of 1755, the lace industry was fostered in the neighbourhood by the Marquis de Pombal as a relief measure.

In the nineteenth century, the women of Peniche, a little peninsula north of Lisbon, achieved fame for their lace work. They worked on wide cylindrical pillows so that the wide lace could be made without joinings. The women sat in pairs with pillows across their knees. The ends of the pillows were supported by low stools. As the demand for their work grew, these women, mainly the wives of fishermen, advanced to the making of both black and white laces. They favoured Maltese geometrical patterns or else large flower designs placed on meshed grounds.

The Mediterranean Shores

During the Middle Ages and well into the sixteenth century, there was a close commercial bond between Europe and the East. This led to the ready interchange of technique and design in all forms of needlework. Patterns favoured by Peruvian tapestry workers and embellished by Rhodian potters were adapted for use by the lace-workers of Southern Europe. In process of time, the graceful arabesques, scrolls and Eastern flower motifs were conveyed to the northern countries of Europe. The vital cross-currents between East and West lent vigour to art in all its forms.

The lace-workers of the Islands of the Aegean practised a simple technique and were content with simple designs. The bobbin-made laces they made were polychrome; the designs were outlined with coloured threads.

The Sicilians devoted much time to the making of lace. The influence of Venice was strong as was also that of Genoa and Milan. Needlepoint evolved by the usual progression from drawn-work and cut-work.

Sardinia produced some attractive and individual laces. One of the most charming was a fine white lace carrying a traditional design. Figure motifs were scattered over the fabric and were enfolded by floral festoons and scrolls. Another attractive filet was made of blue and white threads. The fabric was coarse and the designs conventional.

Malta achieved renown with her laces. The widespread popularity was occasioned not by the quality of the laces but by the fact that they were introduced into the Far East where they were practised assiduously. They were introduced there through the zeal of Christian missionaries. The laces were made so effectively in the Eastern schools that they came to be regarded as examples of native craft. Largely due to the religious aura which surrounded them, Maltese laces were copied in many of the European countries. They were favoured also because they were cheap and durable.

Maltese lace was a guipure lace. Geometrical patterns and arabesques formed the design. The Maltese Cross figured prominently. A distinguishing symbol was that of an oat worked in stitches on the fabric.

The earliest Maltese laces owed much to Greece, the country which has been called the cradle of embroidery. Greek patterns were used and these were worked in thread far finer than that used in later years.

Black lace of an excellent quality was manufactured in Malta. Black and white guipure laces were made in the nineteenth century.

In the Barbary States and in Morocco in particular, embroidery work of a high standard was made. Its influence was far-reaching on the needlework of Europe. It is somewhat disappointing therefore to find that no lace of any excellence was made. The lace made covered a narrow range only. The most popular variety was one worked in a coarse thread; the design was heavy and incorporated many archaic motifs. Next in popularity was a needlepoint lace resembling the *punto avorio* of Italy.

In Turkey much lace was made in the harems. A Grand Turk of the mid-eighteenth century passed sumptuary laws against the wearing of gold lace and he enforced his edicts stringently.

Point de Turquie was known in commerce but a Turkish lace of the nineteenth century was more widely accepted. It was made with the needle and tambour hook in black and in white and in bright colours. Flowers and foliage and fruit were massed together to form designs.

Germany

BARBARA UTTMANN Tradition holds that much of the success of the early lace-workers of Germany was due to the initiative and sustained efforts of Barbara Uttmann, born in 1514, the daughter of a burgher of Nuremberg.

When she was a young girl, she learnt the art of pillow lace from a Brabant Protestant fleeing from the persecutions of the Duke of Alva. She married a rich master miner and went to live in the Harz Mountains of Saxony. There she saw young girls making network caps for the miners. Profiting by her knowledge of bobbin-lace and adept now in the peculiar network of the district, she taught the girls of the neighbourhood how to make a fine knitted tricot and then advanced to the making of a lace ground.

In 1561, Barbara Uttmann set up her own factory at Annaberg. She enlisted help from Flanders and lace in a variety of patterns was made. So successful was this enterprise that it spread into the Bavarian frontier. When the benefactress died in 1575, more than 30,000 persons were employed in the lace industry.

An old sorceress had foretold that St Anne would reward Barbara Uttmann by making her children prosper. Not one of them would die in her lifetime and her descendants would multiply to the number of the bobbins used in the district. When Barbara Uttmann died, she left sixty-five children and great-grandchildren. Her tomb bore the inscription: 'Here lies Barbara Uttmann, died 14 Jan 1575, whose invention of lace in the year 1561 made her the benefactress of the Harz Mountains. An active mind, a skilful hand, bring blessings on the Fatherland.'

Zeal rather than accuracy inspired the inscription. Barbara Uttmann *fostered* the pillow-lace industry of Germany; she did not invent it.

EARLY GERMAN LACES German laces had been in existence in the sixteenth century. The lace-workers learnt the technique from their Flemish neighbours and later they received help from Flemish immigrants who settled in Saxony at the time of the Spanish Inquisition.

French refugees settled in the country in the seventeenth century. Dresden became an important centre. In the eighteenth century there was a high demand for Dresden work, particularly Dresden ruffles. The decade 1760–1770 witnessed a high demand for Dresden needlepoint. Cultural societies established in many countries held Dresden work as the finest example of good workmanship and offered prizes to all who could emulate Dresden work. Dresden aprons and Dresden ruffles were considered essential to a person of fashion. A quotation of *The Fool of Quality*, 1766, reads: 'Smash go the glasses, aboard pours the wine on circling laces, Dresden aprons, silvered silks and rich brocades.'

French emigrants settled in Northern Germany in the seventeenth century and taught the Germans to make the gold and silver laces which were so fashionable. *Hamburg Point* was much in demand. A record of the nineteenth century reads: 'At Hamburg . . . Nelson purchased a magnificent lace trimming for Lady Nelson and a black lace cloak for another lady, who, he said, had been very attentive to his wife during his absence.'

GERMAN LACE CENTRES Berlin attracted many Huguenot artisans. After the Revocation of the Edict of Nantes, the city became an important industrial centre. As many as 450 fabrics were made there. The Prussians had reason to welcome the French artisans settled in their midst. In a short time, laces were being exported to France, Poland and Russia. Other lace centres were at Leipzig, Elberfeld, Halle, Anspach. Hungarian lace was a popular variety. *Point de Hongrie* refers, however, not to lace but to a stitch in tapestry.

EXTRAVAGANCES OF DRESS The Germans dressed simply in the seventeenth century, but in the eighteenth century a reaction amounting to dandyism set in. Extravagances of dress were indulged in to a remarkable degree. The Bishop of Salisbury, writing in 1748, recorded that the students of Leipzig 'think it most honourable to beg, with a sword by their side, of all they meet than to gain a livelihood. I have often given a few groschen to one finely powdered and dressed with sword and lace ruffles'.

In an age of extravagance the luxuries of the German spas were without parallel. The scene at Baden is described in a pamphlet entitled *Merveilleux Amusements des Bains de Bade*. This was published in London in 1739. Bath mantles were trimmed with the richest point. After the bath, each person of fashion spread out his *équipage de bain* as ostentatiously as was possible before the windows. The nobility loitered up and down the streets commenting on the laces in view.

In Saxony during the nineteenth century, men as well as women were employed in the lace industry. Old Brussels point lace was copied and a *dentelle torchon* was made. The work of masculine hands was much sought after for it was stronger and of a more durable quality than that made by women. Lace-work was made at Augsburg and Nuremberg. These included peasant varieties and involved the use of braid in the serpentine designs. Coarse thread was used.

CATERPILLAR LACE At Munich a lace-worker created what was called caterpillar lace. Large hairy insects became all unconsciously lace-makers. A paste of food was spread on a flat stone and with a fine brush dipped in oil, a lace design was spread on the paste. The stone was set upright and the caterpillars were placed at its base. The insects worked their way to the top and ate that food untouched by oil. They spun a strong web as they went and this held the uneaten parts together. The lace thus made was of extraordinary lightness being much lighter than superfine flax thread.

PATTERN BOOKS The German printing presses produced the earliest printed books on lace. At Nuremberg was published in 1601 the model book of Sibmacher. The frontispiece showed a conventional garden of the formal sixteenth-century type. A tree depicted in it bore the dictum 'that she who loves the art of needlework and desires to make herself skilful, can here have it in perfection and she will acquire praise, honour and reward'. A young woman named Industria was seated under the tree. Near her, toying with a large feather, sat Ignavia, or Idleness. Behind stood a portly dame – Sofia, or Wisdom.

A pattern book of earlier date was published in Augsburg in 1534 by John Schwartzenburg. It had many graceful designs, many being borders. Another published by Latomus appeared at Frankfurt-on-Main in 1605. Cologne has the distinction of having published the earliest *dated* pattern book, that of Metrepiere Quinty, published in 1527.

Switzerland

A romantic beginning is given by tradition to the introduction of fine lace-making in Switzerland. In 1572 a certain Symphorien Thelusson, a merchant of Lyons, escaped from the massacre of St Bartholomew by concealing himself in a bale of goods which was carried to Geneva. He was welcomed and found a means of rewarding his hosts by teaching them how to make lace.

When more than a hundred and twenty years had passed, French *émigrés* entered Geneva in bands, for they sought freedom to worship following on the Revocation of the Edict of Nantes. Such was the position and prestige of a descendant of Thelusson, the lace-maker, that he engaged two thousand refugees in his service and established a lace manufactory.

LACE PEDLARS An aureole of romance clung to Swiss lace in its method of disposal. It was carried over the Jura Mountains, along roads and through passes which none but the pedlars knew. They did this in order to evade the duties imposed by the officers of the customs houses of Valence.

Much of the lace made in Switzerland was of the guipure type. Country women made considerable quantities of it as they watched their flocks.

The main centre of the lace-making industry was Neufchâtel and work resembling the finest done in Flanders was sometimes created there. The Val-de-Travers was another lace-making area.

ROUSSEAU ON LACE-MAKING When at Moutiers, Jean Jacques Rousseau endeavoured to make some bobbin lace. He recommended lace-making as a suitable occupation for women (*Emile*, Book IV):

'But what Sophie knows best, and has been more thoroughly trained to, is work special to her own sex, such as cutting out and making up dresses. There is no needlework in which she is not adept, knowing how to do it well, and doing it with pleasure, but that which she prefers above others is lace-making, because it necessitates a pretty attitude and provides an exercise for the fingers which involves more grace and lightness of touch.'

PATTERN BOOKS Switzerland, like Germany, can claim the distinction of issuing early pattern books. In 1593, at St Gall, appeared the *New Model Buch* of G. Straub. It owed much to Vecellio's *Corona*. At Basel, in 1599, at the printing house of Ludwig Kunigs, appeared another pattern book entitled *Sehr Newe Model Buch*. Another published at Zürich by Christopher Froschowern has an informative preface:

'Amongst the different arts we must not forget one which has been followed in our country for twenty-five years. Lace-making was introduced in 1536 by merchants from Italy and Venice.

'Many women, seeing a means of livelihood in such work, quickly learnt it and reproduced lace with great skill. They first copied old patterns but soon were enabled to invent new ones of great beauty.

'The industry spread itself through the country and was carried to great perfection; it was found to be one specially suitable for women and brought in good profits.

'In the beginning, these laces were used solely for trimming chemises and shirts; soon afterwards collars, trimmings for cuffs, caps and fronts and bodies of dresses, for napkins, sheets, pillow-cases and coverlets, etc., were made in lace. Very soon such lace was in great demand and became an article of great luxury.

'Gold thread was subsequently introduced into some of it, and raised its value considerably; but this latter sort was attended with the inconvenience that it was more difficult to clean and wash than laces made with flax thread only.'

Denmark

Opinion is divided as to the manner in which lace-craft was introduced into Denmark. Some give the credit to a band of monks seeking refuge in the country at the time of the Reformation; others maintain that it was introduced by Queen Elizabeth, sister of Charles V and wife of Christian II.

CHRISTIAN IV PATRON OF LACE The native lace industries were carefully fostered by Christian IV. His portrait by Peeter Isaakoz is fairly well known and shows him wearing an elaborate lace collar as a trimming for the rich dress of the period.

A lace-maker, a young girl, had the good fortune of finding, in 1639, the Golden Horn, one of the chief treasures of the Scandinavian Museum. Christian IV rewarded her.

Lace-making was never an important source of revenue in Denmark. South Jutland only established the industry on a regular basis.

TÖNDER LACE The year 1647 ushered in an important epoch in the lace industry of Jutland. A merchant named Steenbeck established at Tönder twelve lace teachers from Dortmund in Westphalia. The twelve were aged men wearing long beards. These they gathered into bags to prevent them becoming entangled in the bobbins. Young and old, rich and poor, came to be taught. Soon Tönder lace experienced a wide reputation and the lace-making area extended to the south-western part of Ribe and to the island of Romo.

LACE POSTMEN The lace was sold by 'lace postmen' who carried their wares to all parts of Scandinavia and Germany. As the name implies, the system was carried on with considerable regularity and method. The lace trade was thus not in the hands of casual pedlars; the lace postmen were an organized band, under direct supervision of the lace merchants, at a time when the perils of the road were considerable.

Jens Wulff, one of the foremost promoters of the lace industry in Denmark, travelled far as a lace postman. His son, describing him, said:

'My late father who began the lace trade of the last century [nineteenth] first went on foot with his wares to Mecklenburg, Prussia and Hanover; we consigned lace to all parts of the world.

'Soon he could afford to buy a horse; and in his old age, he calculated he had travelled on horseback more than 75,000 English miles, or thrice round the earth.

'In his youth, the most durable and prettiest ground was the old Flemish, much used by the peasants of Germany. It was solid and passed as an heirloom through several generations. Later, the fine needleground came in and lastly the *fond clair*, or *Point de Lille*, far less solid but easier to work; hence the lace-makers became less skilful than of old.'

The lace-makers at Tönder were conservative in their designs. The most expert workers spent their lives in the creation of one pattern only. Among the more popular patterns were feather, cock-eye, chimney-pot, spider and lyre.

A marked decline set in about 1830. Up to that time Tönder lace had been made in the best flax or in the finest silk thread.

Cotton thread was now used and the lace was far less durable. Lace-making became a subsidiary industry following on the growth and prosperity of agriculture.

Sweden

THE CONVENT OF VADSTENA St Bridget (d. 1335) is reputed to have introduced the art of lace-making into the convent of Vadstena on her return from Italy. In an old portrait of this saint taken after death in Rome, she is wearing a coif edged with a species of early cut-work, or lacis.

In the Middle Ages, the nuns of Vadstena 'Knit their laces of gold and silk'.

According to the rules of the convent, the nuns at Vadstena were not allowed to touch gold or silver except in their needlework. It is disappointing to find on examination of an old journal of the Kloster, *Diarium Vadstenonse*, no reference to the needlework made in the convent. An old collection of documents, *Vadstena Past and Present* (Förr och Nu), contains an informative letter written by one of the nuns to her lover who lived in the town.

'I wish', writes the nun, 'I could send you a netted cap that I myself have made, but when Sister Karin Andersdotter saw that I have mingled gold and silver thread in it, she said, "You must surely have some beloved."

' "Do not think so," I answered. "Here in the Kloster you may easily see if any of the brethren has such a cap, and I dare not send it by any one to a sweetheart outside the walls."

' "You intend it for Axel Nilson," answered Sister Karin.

' "It is not for you to talk," I replied. "I have seen you net a long hood and talk and prattle yourself with Brother Bertol." '

When Charles IX suppressed the religious houses, many of the nuns took refuge in Poland. Some of the oldest nuns remained in Sweden and maintained themselves by making lace. Many of the secrets of the craft which they had guarded zealously now became known to the populace.

Vadstena lace was used to trim the national costume. Törchon lace was made and used extensively for the splendid drawn-work bed linen on which the Swedish families prided themselves.

Hölesom, or cut-work, was a favourite form of embroidery in Sweden.

Vadstena was the only centre for lace-making, but much lace was made by the peasantry. The peasant laces of Dalescarlia were well known. They were worn, heavily starched, on the summer caps of married women and served as a protection against the sun. The lace-makers of Orsa specialized in the making of laces of unbleached thread. Narrow 'seaming' laces were made at Rattvik; the design usually favoured was the lozenge. A lace resembling Genoese macrame was also made and was used for bed trimming.

Among the national treasures preserved at Stockholm are personal possessions of Gustavus Adolphus. One is a lace collar bearing the inscription:

'This collar was worn by Gustaf Adolf, King of Sweden, and presented, together with his portrait, as a remembrance in 1632 to Miss Jacobina Lauber of Augsburg because she was the most beautiful lady present.'

Heroism characterizes the other treasure, the blood-stained shirt worn by Gustavus at the Battle of Dirschau. The collar and cuffs are trimmed with lace of rich geometrical pattern. The sleeves are decorated with 'seaming' lace.

Russia

Russia concentrated on embroidery; lace-making always remained a subservient craft. Lace made there was coarse and the designs had an Oriental character.

Peter the Great founded a lace factory at Novgorod. Catherine II employed twelve gold lace-workers at St Petersburg.

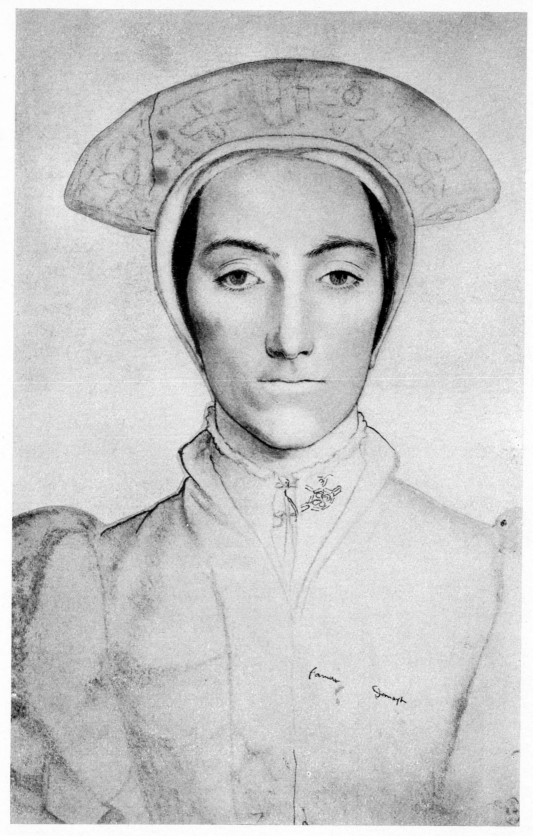

Portrait of a Lady Unknown. Hans Holbein
Drawing at Windsor Castle. The head-dress shows early drawn work

England. Sampler panel of needlepoint lace
First half of the seventeenth century

Queen Elizabeth

The ruff is edged with Venetian needlepoint

English lace. Buckinghamshire. Shawl of bobbin lace
First half of the nineteenth century
Length: 10 feet 9 inches. Width: 4 feet 10½ inches

THE LACES OF BRITAIN

I N the early Middle Ages, Englishwomen were renowned for their needlework. *Opus Anglicanum* achieved international fame. Much of the fine embroidery was used for ecclesiastical purposes. Devoted women felt a spiritual vocation in creating handwork of lasting grace and delicacy.

CHURCH EMBROIDERY As in the early Anglo-Saxon Church, so too in the Norman English Church, it was the practice to place movable frontals on the altar. This custom continued down to the Reformation, and it reflects on the patience and industry of the women of Britain that when the order came for the dispensation of such church furnishings, every parish church could boast a complete set of hangings and frontals for the altar. When the stone altars were removed to give way to wooden tables by command of Queen Elizabeth in 1565, much of the needlework made to adorn the church disappeared. Some, however, was treasured up in old chests in the churches, and it is from these that one may garner knowledge concerning the nature of early ecclesiastical vestments and furnishings. Rich needlework, including bands of gold lace and thread lace, featured on most garments and cloths. Again and again one sighs with disappointment that so much exquisite work, resting for centuries in damp repositories has been open to attack from damp, for much exquisite work has been destroyed or defaced by mould. It is evident that Englishwomen had achieved a high standard of skill in 'lacies' and cut-work, but despite the high standard of work in these varieties of needlework, no internationally recognized reputation for early 'lacies' was attained.

EARLY PILLOW LACE The pillow lace industry of England became established with the infiltration of Flemish women into the country in the fifteenth century. Knowledge of lace-making can be traced before that time. Chaucer, writing his Prologue to the *Canterbury Tales* in the latter half of the fourteenth century, described the purse of the carpenter as 'purled with latoun'. This was a wire lace, usually gold or silver coloured. In 1363, Edward III signed an Act of Parliament controlling the use of veils which women wore as cauls. These veils were edged with a simple lace border. The Great Wardrobe Account of 1347 records a charge for 12,000 pins for the trousseau of Joanna, Edward's daughter. These pins were required for the making of pillow lace. Two Harleian MSS., dating *circa* 1471, refer to the making of bobbin or pillow laces. One of these is of interest as referring to the types of laces prevalent in the reigns of Henry VI and Edward IV. It claims that it gives 'directions for making many sorts of laces'. These include 'Lace Bascon, Lace endented, Lace bordred on both syde, yn o syde, pykke lace bordred, Lace Condrak, Lace Dawns, Lace Piol, Lace covert, Lace coverte doble, Lace compon coverte, Lace maskel, Lace cheyne brode, Las Cheveron, Lace ounde, Grene dorge, Lace for Hattys Etc.' An interesting feature of the MS. is that the illuminated capital which begins the subject-matter, shows the figure of a woman employed in what was probably one of these arts. The illustration is damaged but the process appears to be based on a form of cardweaving. The work was done with the hands, the fingers carrying the thread so that a form of open-work lace or braid was formed. This process marked an advance on methods employed in creating gold and silver *passementerie* from cords and lacings which early writers refer to collectively as 'lace'.

The Wardrobe Accounts of Edward IV lists under *Total of stuffs bought*: 'Laces made of ryban of silk; two dozen laces and a double lace of ryban; corses of sylk with laces and tassels of silk.' The double laces referred to plaiting. He made payment to Alice Claver, his sylkwoman for 'two dozen laces and a double lace of sylk'.

LACE WORN IN ENGLAND IN THE MIDDLE AGES Lace, in its modern significance, was worn by the Queen of Richard III – 'whyte silk and Venys gold'. The King's saddle of cloth of gold was ornamented with 'netts and rooses' and his doublet was trimmed with 'netts and pyne appels', this being in all probability an early Venetian guipure lace, the tie bars or brides of which were too exquisite for detailed description at the hands of the accountant of the Royal Wardrobe Accounts. At his coronation the King wore a robe of crimson satin, 'laced with two laces of ryban and laces of sylke'.

In the reign of Richard III there was proclaimed a prohibition against the wearing of lace. Earlier, in 1454, a protest was made against the settlement of six women, who were probably Flemish, on the ground that they were training Englishwomen in the linen and darning work of the Low Countries. It was thought that the practice would prove detrimental to English forms of needlework. In view of the prestige of the Englishwomen and their dexterity, it is altogether surprising that at this time they did not endeavour to attain great skill in the making of needlepoint lace, taking the exquisite work of Italy as their models.

LACE IN THE TUDOR PERIOD Gold and silver lace was imported into England in considerable quantities in the reign of Henry VII. The King himself spent a considerable sum on 'gold of Venys, gold of Danmarke'. Queen Elizabeth of York purchased on many occasions 'laces and rybans' and 'hosyn laces ryban and sope'. The Keeper of the Great Wardrobe warranted an order in the eighteenth year of the King's reign 'for the use and wearing of our right dere dauther the Lady Mary . . . a black velvet gown, a scarlet petticoat and a nounce of lace for her kyrtel and a thousand pynnes.' At the same time was issued a warrant for 'a mauntel lace of blewe silk and Venys gold, to be delivered for the use of our right dere and well-beloved Cosyn, the King of Romayne'. This was a present to Maximilian on the occasion of his being made a Knight of the Garter.

An inventory of the King's plate which was made in his son's reign in 1543, makes reference to the term lace but gives no exact meaning to it.

'*Item*, oone picture of a woman made of erthe, with a carnacon Roobe knitt with a knot in the lefte shoulder and bare hedid with her heere rowlid up with a white lace sett in a box of wodde.

'*Item*, oone picture of a woman made of erthe, with a carnacon garment after the Inglishe tyer and bareheddid with her heare rowled up with a white lace sett in a box of wodde.'

HENRY VIII Lace was used in ever-growing quantities in the reign of Henry VIII. The Privy Purse expenses show that in 1530 the King paid to Richard Cecyll, Groom of the Robes (and father of Lord Burleigh) five shillings and eight-pence for eight pieces of 'yolowe lace, bought for the King's Grace'. Also listed are 'green silk lace' and '8 pieces of yellow lace, 9s 4d'.

The 'Acts of Apparell' of the realm forbade the importation of foreign laces, but in 1546 these acts were waived aside, for Henry granted a licence to two merchants from Florence to export for a lease of three years, 'all manner of fryngys and passements wrought with gold and silver or otherwise and all other new gentillesses of what facyn or value soever they may be, for the pleasure of our dearest wyeff the Queen, our nobles, gentlemen and others.'

The wife of the time was Catherine Parr, but she, like the other women of her age, was content with 'perle edgings' to her coif.

AN EARLY PORTRAIT SHOWING LACIS Mention must be made here of an inventory of 1519 which refers to an article called the 'laced linen of Holland' and to a 'yard of lace'. At Windsor Castle hangs a drawing of a woman by Hans Holbein. An illustration of this is included in this volume by gracious permission of H.M. The Queen. Exact identification of the portrait is not known, though for long general opinion has accredited it with being that of Anne of Cleves, wife of Henry VIII. The evidence put forward in support of this is that the artist made the drawing in July 1539 when he journeyed to Düren to paint a portrait of Henry's prospective bride. Some think, on the other hand, that the portrait is that of Amelia, the sister of Anne. Be that as it may, the head-dress worn is relative to the date indicated. The coif is shown as white and is suggestive of linen. Its decoration is a band of lettered drawn-work, a form of needlework much favoured at the time. It is noteworthy that a design very similar to that shown in the Holbein drawing and entitled the 'libertas piece' was shown in a pattern book by Vavassore which was published in 1532.

QUEEN CATHERINE AND THE BEDFORDSHIRE LACE INDUSTRY When Henry's ill-fated Queen, Catherine of Aragon, retired to Ampthill in Bedfordshire in 1531, pending her appeal to Rome, she is said to have fostered the art of lace-making as a means of sub-sistence for the peasantry. Catherine herself was an expert needlewoman, having been trained by her mother, Queen Isabelle of Spain. There is a well-known anecdote which tells how Wolsey and the papal legate, Campeggio, went to Bridewell to discuss the matter of divorce with the Queen and found her, like ancient Penelope, surrounded by her maidens and engaged in needlework. The Queen went forward to meet the Cardinal with a skein of red silk around her neck.

Catherine, during her three years' sojourn at Ampthill, 'passed her time, when not at her devotions, with her gentlewomen, working with her own hands, something wrought in needlework, costly and artificially, which she intended for the honour of God to bestow on some of the churches'. There is, doubtless, a strong element of truth in the local folk-lore of Bedfordshire wherein it is maintained that 'the country-people began to love her exceedingly. They visited her out of pure respect and she received the tokens of regard they daily showed her most sweetly and graciously'. In return, Catherine taught them the art of pillow lace and thus laid, in part, the foundations of the Bedford lace industry which was to flourish for three centuries. For long the lace-makers honoured November 25th as Cattern's Day, 'in memory of good Queen Catherine who, when the trade was dull, burnt all her lace and ordered new to be made. The ladies of the court followed her example and the fabric once more revived.' The lace-workers of Kettering, Northamptonshire, honoured the memory of Queen Catherine as patroness of their craft by the custom of preparing and eating Cattern cakes.

FLORENTINE LACE MERCHANTS When King Henry granted the special licence to the Italian merchants he claimed as his right the privilege of having a pre-view of their merchandise and of selecting those things which pleased him. There is no documentary evidence that he purchased anything for Catherine Parr, who, like Henry's first Catherine, was an expert and industrious needlewoman. She, too, had been instructed in the art by her mother. An old astrologer visiting her home, foretold that she would become a queen. The young Catherine, so legend tells, threw down her needlework, exclaiming: 'My hands are ordained to touch crowns and sceptres, not needles and spindles.'

Henry purchased from the Florentines 'trunk sleeves of redd cloth of gold with cut-work; handkerchers edged with gold and silver; knitted gloves of silk; diaper towels "with Stafford Knots" and "Knots and roses" '; handkerchiefs of Holland 'frynged with gold of Venys, redd and white silk'; 'coverpanes of fyne diaper of Adam and Eve garnished about with a narrow passamayne of Venice gold and silver'.

Lace was used lavishly for church purposes. White-work and cut-work adorned surplices and altar frontals.

Inventories such as that of St Mary-at-Hill, London, show that lace trimmed church linen.

QUEEN MARY'S REVIVAL OF SUMPTUARY LAWS Queen Mary Tudor revived the sumptuary laws of her father. These were reinforced in the first and second years of her reign. Their main purpose was to regulate the amount and the nature of foreign cut-work imported into Britain and to establish a social scale regarding its use. Barons and men of higher rank were allowed to trim their personal clothing with this form of needlework; likewise, the wife of a knight or a lady of higher rank might use it as a trimming. To all others, the use of wreath lace and passement, lace of gold and silver with sleeves, partlet or linen trimmed with purles of gold and silver or whiteworks, alias whiteworks and similar works from across the seas was strictly forbidden. Lace at this period was called by many names – passemayne, purles, bone-work.

Under the Plantagenet kings, Britain had been interested primarily in the laces of the Low Countries. As the Tudor period progressed, this interest was transferred to Spanish tastes. Spanish work is often referred to in the inventories of Henry VIII, and this preference for Spanish modes deepened in the reign of Queen Mary Tudor and her Spanish consort, Philip II. Queen Elizabeth showed a preference for French and Italian fashions, and this interest prevailed through the succeeding Stuart period.

ELABORATE RUFFS The European custom of wearing ruffs penetrated into Britain in the reign of Philip and Mary. The vogue grew under Elizabeth. Ruffs were adorned with elaborate points in geometric pattern. These were prized by the nobles but were decried by the austere preachers of the Reformation. Towards the close of Elizabeth's reign, it was usual to colour needlepoint lace with saffron. Venetian points were imported in large quantities.

Lord Bacon, in his *Advice to Sir George Villiers*, wrote: 'Our English dames are much given to the wearing of costly laces, and if brought from Italy and Flanders, they are much in esteem, whereas if like laces were made by the English, so much thread would make a yard of lace, being put into that manufacture would be five times or perhaps ten or twenty times the value.'

QUEEN ELIZABETH Queen Elizabeth favoured a ruff of large size, as is shown in many of her portraits. For a time, she appears to have had exclusive rights to the art of starching, this being known to the Dutch wife of her coachman, Gwyllan Boenen. It was rumoured that the Queen wore such large ruffs, 'chin ruffs', because of her desire to conceal her 'yellow throat'. Finest cut-work adorned these collars which were ornamented with gold and silver and precious stones. Though indulging in three-tiered ruffs herself, she did not extend the privilege of wearing them to her courtiers.

Various Acts were passed in Elizabeth's reign with a view to suppressing extravagances in dress. Nevertheless the Great Wardrobe Accounts and the New Years' Gifts relative to Elizabeth testify to her own costly and elaborate tastes. Her petticoats were trimmed with gold lace or with bone lace of Venys silver. There are curious entries referring to 'doublets of peche satten all over covered with cut-work and lyned with a lace of Venyse gold, kyrtells of white satten embroidered with purles of gold like clouds and layed round about with a bond lace of Venys gold'. There were numerous entries in the inventories of Elizabeth's possessions referring to laces of Jean and Spanish lace, bone lace of copper and bone lace of copper and silver.

Some of the lace was made in England. A certain William Bowll provided the Queen with 'lace of crowne purle'. She paid her silkwoman, Alice Montague, nine shillings for making bone lace wrought with silver and with spangles.

The fashion for wearing aprons in full dress appeared in this reign and continued down to the eighteenth century. Handkerchiefs, lace-trimmed, were also a novelty. These were at first about three to four inches square and their prime purpose was to serve as love tokens.

The majority of entries in the Great Wardrobe Accounts testify to the fact that Elizabeth was not sufficiently patriotic to foster the lace-makers of Britain and bestow on them royal patronage at the expense of foreign lace-makers. She obtained her cut-work and laces from all countries and also from whatever sources possible. There is something nauseating in the thought of her action in pillaging the French finery of Mary, Queen of Scots, on its way to the unfortunate Queen in prison. Elizabeth selected and retained for her own use those articles of dress and adornment which she fancied.

EARLY SETTLEMENTS OF FOREIGN ARTISANS Royal proclamations were made against 'excess of luxury in wearing apparel', and Acts were passed to suppress the wearing of 'silk glittering with silver and gold lace'. In harmony with this policy of stringency, Elizabeth refused in the year 1572 to allow Flemish artisans to find refuge in England. Those that did arrive were forcibly expelled from the country. Foreign lace-makers had already established themselves, however, in England, particularly in remote districts in the south-eastern area. The census of the City of London dated 1571 gives a list of aliens. Of the four thousand two hundred and eighty-seven resident, four were lace-makers. One of these was named Callys de Hove of Burgundy, and the other 'Mary Jurdaine, widow, of the French nation and maker of purled lace'.

Despite this lack of official hospitality, lace-makers among other artisans continued to filter into the country. In Britain, as in several other countries, lace-making owed its real inspiration to foreigners. Waves of Continental refugees flowed into different areas of the country. One of the earliest settlements had been made as far back as 1563 when, following on the ruthlessness of the Spanish Inquisition, Protestants from the Low Countries settled along the coasts of Kent. Some of these were skilled in the making of 'parchment' lace. They taught their art to the people among whom they settled. A further influx came in 1568; these refugees came from Mechlin and the surrounding district. These refugees did not settle in Kent but moved inland and laid the foundations of the lace industry which was to thrive in later centuries. The refugees made their homes in Bedfordshire, Buckinghamshire and Northamptonshire, where the thriving lace centres of the Midland counties were to be established later. A third mass migration occurred in 1572 resulting from the slaughter of the Huguenots of France. Many of the immigrants were skilled lace-makers and their coming infused new zeal and inspiration into the lace-workers already at work in England.

The geometric or reticello type of work was still favoured and this continued well into the reign of James I. The standard of work was not sufficiently high to gain for English lace international – or even national – recognition. The laces of the Low Countries and of Italy were still imported in vast bales, for they were needed for elaborate neck-ruffs, for voluminous gowns and doublets, and for trimmings for jackets of cloth and of velvet and also for caps, aprons, kerchiefs and handkerchiefs.

POINT TRESSE The Elizabethan period witnessed a vogue for *Point Tresse*. This was lace made from human hair. Accounts, rendering the expenses of Queen Elizabeth, frequently make reference to this variety. Lace made from hair was not an innovation. It appears to have derived its origin from the romantic days of chivalry. It is recorded in the *Chevalier aux ij Epées* that a noble lady asked King Ris to present her with a mantle bearing a fringe made from the beards of nine conquered kings and hemmed with that of King Arthur who as yet remained unconquered. An inventory of the embroidery of Mary, Queen of Scots, made at Chartley, mentions: *Un petit quarré fait à point tresse ouvré par la vieille Comtesse de Lenoux, elle estant à la Tour*. This gift, bestowed by the mother of Darnley, seems to exonerate the Queen in the eyes of the family from the implication of murder.

The technique of making *Point Tresse* was known on the Continent. Elderly lace-workers made it from their own hair. Lace of this fabric was comparatively rare and commanded high prices. At his coronation in 1614, Louis XIV wore a cravat made of silvery white hair. The cravat was soon to become an essential part of the costume of both men and women. It was adopted as an eminently suitable vehicle for lace fabric. The wearers forgot the origin of the cravat. The Cravates, or Croates, had in early times worn neck-bands to support amulets which they believed protected them from sabre-cuts. In the eighteenth and nineteenth centuries Dalecarlian peasant girls excelled above all others in the making of *Point Tresse*, and it was an easy transition to the making of wigs at which they excelled.

EARLY ENGLISH LACES The Stuart period witnessed an advance in the lace-making industry of Britain. The lace produced supplied a home market. The English lace-workers went to the lace-workers of Venice for inspiration. The demand of the age was for lace with elaborate points. This gave way towards the middle of the century to a desire for broad rounded scallops which in turn gave place to the straight-edged variety in the closing years of the same century. The pattern makers of the time developed the foliated scrolls which were reminiscent of Venetian designs.

ANTAGONISM OF THE REFORMED CHURCH The paintings of the early Stuart era and the numerous monuments in cathedrals and churches are valuable as records of the lace-work of the time, for artists delighted in depicting the geometric designs in detail. In vain did the dignitaries of the Church of England pour down anathemas on the extravagances of fashion. The Bishop of Exeter was no visionary, even if he was a powerful preacher, when in the early seventeenth century he decried the lace industry which was to be of such great economic worth in his diocese for centuries.

'But if none of our persuasions can prevail, hear this, ye garish popinjays of our time,' he cried, 'if ye will not be ashamed to clothe yourselves after this shameless fashion, Heaven shall clothe you with shame and confusion.

'Hear this, ye plaister-faced Jezebels, if ye will not leave your daubs and washes, Heaven will one day wash them off with fire and brimstone.'

That dignitary whom James I was pleased to call 'the King of Preachers' – John King, Bishop of London, declaimed with vituperation:

'Fashion has brought in deep ruffs and shallow ruffs, thick ruffs, and thin ruffs, double ruffs and no ruffs. When the Judge of the quick and the dead shall appear, he will not know those who have so defaced the fashion he hath created.'

The richness of dress had an economic significance, often costing its wearer the greater part of the income of his estate. In 1599 Ben Jonson wrote in *Every Man out of his Humour* that the nobles thought little of 'turning four or five hundred acres of their best land into two or three trunks of apparel'.

When Queen Elizabeth died, James I rode down the length of Britain from Scotland. When he reached London, he arranged with the English Privy Council that a quantity of the deceased Queen's gowns, mantles and ruffs should be forwarded to his wife, Anne of Denmark, because of the poverty of her wardrobe which was wholly inappropriate for a regal entry into the metropolis. The masculine arrangement concerning feminine attire courted disaster. Anne, young, beautiful, vivacious – she was barely twenty-six years old – discarded the rich clothing of the seventy-year-old Queen as soon as she reached London.

ENGLISH LACES FAVOURED When she selected her own dresses, she showed herself to be very patriotic. The courtiers patronized the laces of Italy and the Low Countries but Anne, heroically and defiantly, bought the laces of Britain. At Winchester and at Basing she bought quantities of 'Great Bone Lace' and 'Little Bone Lace', and these varieties feature largely in memoranda of her expenses.

At the birth of the Princess Sophia in 1606, the Queen purchased lace to the value of £614 5s 8d. No mention is made that any of the laces were imported from foreign countries. It was usual to specify the place of manufacture, and so one may infer that the laces were made in Britain. The little princess lived only three days. When her little monument was placed in the chapel of Henry VII in Westminster Abbey, it was in the form of a small cradle with coverlet and sheets trimmed with lace. On her marriage, Anne's daughter, the Princess Elizabeth, was provided with, according to the Warrant on the Great Wardrobe 1612–13, 'gold cheine laze, silver spangled, silver looped, myllen bone lace, drawne-worke poynte, black silk Naples lace' and with silver bone lace amounting to the astonishing total of 1,692 ounces.

CHARLES I During the reign of Charles I, lace fabrics were used with ever-growing extravagance. An indication of their prolific use is seen from an entry in the King's Wardrobe Accounts which refers to 994 yards of lace for twelve collars and for 24 pairs of lace cuffs. Later 600 yards of lace were required for trimming the ruffs attached to the King's night-clothes.

FALLING COLLAR Ruffs were gradually ousted in this reign, their place being taken by the falling collar. This formed a beautiful and characteristic feature of the gorgeous Cavalier costume. These collars were decorated with geometric cut-work and bone-work. Some of this was produced in Britain for the lace industry was growing.

EARLY EXPORT OF LACE It is significant of this strong activity that in 1620 one of the thriving English trading companies exported large quantities of gold and silver lace made in this country to India for the use of the King of Galconda.

The pillow lace of Britain was gaining a sound reputation in France also. In 1636, Henrietta Maria sent a casket of laces and other fashionable trimmings to Anne of Austria. The high value set on English lace is apparent from a letter written on May 18th, 1637, by the Countess of Leicester who was forwarding a quantity of the fabric to the Queen of France. She wrote to her husband:

'All my present for the Queen of France is provided, which I have done with great care and some trouble: the expenses I cannot yet directly tell you, but I think it will be about £120, for the bone laces are extremely dear.

'I intend to send it to Monsieur Ruvigny, for most of the things are of new fashion, and if I should keep them they would be less acceptable, for what is new now will quickly become common, such things being sent over almost every week.'

STUART FASHIONS Since the Reformation lace-work for Church use had disappeared, almost entirely, but in the reign of Charles I there was a slight revival of the use of lace for ecclesiastical purposes. The search warrants against the Jesuit priests led to the confiscation of lace-trimmed vestments.

LACE FANS There was a growing fashion in this reign to trim articles of toilet lavishly with lace. Cut-work, laces of gold, silver and thread trimmed towels, sheets, cushions and clothing. Men and women carried fans. These were often costly, the leaves being of exquisite lace and the sticks frequently studded with precious stones.

Men had carried fans in the reign of Henry VIII. 'The gentlemen had prodigious fans and they had handles at least half a yard long; with these their daughters were oft-times corrected.' Judges and similar officials carried fans when they served in ill-ventilated rooms. It was for their aesthetic value, however, that the courtiers of the Stuart period carried fans. Not only were the mounts made of fine lace but beautiful edgings were attached to the upper edges of the mounts and at intervals across the span.

Queen Elizabeth sent as a gift to Queen Louise of Lorraine a fan valued at 1,200 crowns. She herself had a fan valued at £400. She issued a decree to her subjects saying that the Sovereign of England was above accepting gifts from subjects. A fan was the only token which might be presented, and this law remained for many centuries.

Fan leaves were an excellent medium for showing the art of the lace-maker. A collection of fans will show the prevailing fashions of the time they were made, for they reflect the tastes in vogue.

LACE IN COMMERCE During the Tudor period lace was sold by pedlars, and the custom lasted into the second half of the seventeenth century. The lace-box was also carried into country inns by the lace-worker herself. In a play written by John Heywood in 1544, a pedlar's box contained 'Laces knotted, laces round and flat for women's heads, sleeve laces'. The lace-pedlar must have been a usual figure on the poorly conditioned roads of England, for in *The Fool of Quality* a murdered pedlar is described as having a box filled with 'silk, linen and laces'.

In the time of Queen Elizabeth, however, much lace was being sold in general stores. The so-called lower classes were now frequent purchasers of lace. At the shop of John Forbeck in Durham could be bought 'velvet lace, coloured silk chagne lace, petticoat lace and Venys gold'. At Darlington, in the shop of John Johnston, there was for sale, 'loom lace', black silk lace and 'statute lace'.

In the Stuart period mercers, in especial, took an interest in the selling of lace fabrics. The courtiers purchased at the establishments but the bulk of the country was pleased to buy at the fairs where the lace-makers were content with smaller profits. As it was at the fair that the native lace-worker sold her wares, patronage at these centres of commerce resulted indirectly in the fostering of home industries.

EARLY SMUGGLING Illegal trading forms a prominent and romantic feature in the history of lace. The smuggling of lace which was to develop on so vast a scale was already evident in the reign of the second Stuart king. The Domestic Papers of 1621 record how a certain Nicholas Peeter, master of the *Greyhound at Apsom*, had landed at Dover and had not declared to the Customs his packages of cut-works and bone-laces.

DECLINE OF USE OF LACE IN THE TIME OF THE COMMONWEALTH The Commonwealth meant a temporary decline in the lace-making industries of Britain. The middle and lower classes, in particular, were governed by severe austerity in dress. The emphasis on Puritan simplicity has, however, been so much emphasized that it has been overrated. Facts and accounts refute an all-pervading austerity. The middle and lower classes used, it is true, but little bobbin lace, and *their* urgings for an age of simplicity bore, at least, the stamp of practical sincerity. The upper classes gave lip service to what had become a party cry which they, in theory, acclaimed in that it represented the spirit of reaction against Royalist extravagance and profligacy.

USE OF LACE BY THE UPPER CLASSES Many members of the upper classes, powerful under Cromwell, disdained the simple Roundhead costume and clung tenaciously to the rich dress of the court of Charles. Sir Thomas Fairfax, the father of General Fairfax, wore a falling collar of lace which hung over his breastplate. His buff coat was trimmed with silver lace and his trunk hose had decorations of expensive Flanders lace. Cromwell's mother possessed a green velvet cloak edged with wide gold lace and handkerchiefs trimmed with broad point lace. Once he had attained supreme power, Cromwell showed a meticulous delight in fine clothes. At his death his body was decked in purple velvet trimmed with ermine and costly Flanders lace. His effigy resplendent with fine laces, overshadowed in splendour that of any monarch.

REACTION IN THE RESTORATION PERIOD The Restoration saw an efflorescence of the fine arts. Luxury and extravagance returned to Britain in full tide. The extravagant ostentation in dress, characteristic of the Stuart period, encouraged the lace-workers. The Wardrobe Accounts reveal the lavish use of lace as a trimming for ruffles, fichus, collars and cuffs. In 1661, Charles II issued a proclamation which re-enforced an Act passed by his father in 1635 prohibiting 'the importation of foreign purles, cut-workes and bone-laces'. Another Act was passed in 1662 prohibiting the purchase of foreign laces. The practice had arisen of smuggling lace from France.

Had Charles himself observed the Acts of prohibition they might have proved effective, but people followed the royal example and continued to buy foreign laces. Dutch influences prevailed. Laces made specially for the royal house often featured motifs showing feathers, oak branches and acorns and the royal crown variously inscribed and all symbolic of the Stuart house.

The custom of wearing flowing wigs and flowing curls became usual. This ended the life of the falling collar which had by now diminished so much in size that it resembled a narrow band. This was worn tied in a loose knot at the front of the neck. The plain cambric slips worn by the clergy and lawyers remain as mementoes of this fashion. With the curled wigs, men wore lace cravats, a vogue which was retained in favour until 1735 when a black bow came into fashion. Accessory to lace cravats were lace gloves. The diarist Evelyn records the custom of presenting 'laced gloves' to a judge presiding at a Maiden Assize. The same writer in 1661 described in *Tyrannus; or the Mode* the current fashion in feminine attire.

> Another quilted white and red,
> With a broad Flanders lace below;
> Four pairs of bas de soye shot through
> With silver; diamond buckles too,
> For garters, and as rich for shoe.
> Twice twelve day smocks of Holland fine
> With cambric sleeves rich Poynt to joyn
> (For she despises Colbertine)
> Twelve more for night, all Flandres lac'd
> Or else she thinks herself disgrac'd.
> The same her night-gown must adorn,
> With Point waistcoats for the morn;
> Of pocket mouchoirs, nose to drain,
> A dozen laced, a dozen plain:
> Three nightgowns of rich Indian stuff;
> Four cushin-cloths are scarce enough
> Of Point and Flanders.

Another famous diarist, Pepys, wrote in his diary, October 19, 1662: 'Put on my new lace band and so neat it is that I am resolved my great expense shall be lace bands and it will set off anything else the more.'

Earlier in the same year, on May 21, he entered: 'My wife and I to my Lord's lodging; where she and I staid walking in White Hall Gardens. And in the Privy Garden saw the finest smock and linnen petticoats of my Lady Castlemaine's laced with rich lace at the bottom, that ever I saw; and it did me good to look at them.'

WILLIAM AND MARY The reign of William and Mary witnessed a further effort to protect English laces. An edict was passed in 1698 prohibiting the importation of foreign laces. This measure reacted so disastrously on the trade of the woolstaplers that the Act was repealed to the extent of admitting laces from the Low Countries. Dutch influences permeated generally throughout the reign and permeated into the lace industry. The result was not altogether unfortunate. English lace-workers were called in to supply the demand for lace. Much lace was required for the fashionable head-dress, the *fontange* which was known as a *commode* in England. Under William and Mary greater sums than ever before were being spent in the purchase of lace.

The lace bill of Queen Mary, which was signed by Lady Derby, Mistress of the Robes for the year 1694, totalled the vast sum of £1,918. Among the more expensive items scheduled were:

	£	s	d
21 yards of lace for 12 pillow beres at 52s	54	12	0
16 yards of lace for 2 toylights at £12	192	0	0
24 yards of lace for 6 handkerchiefs at £4 10s	108	0	0
30 yards of lace for 6 night shifts at 62s	93	0	0
6 yards of lace for 2 combing cloths at £14	84	0	0
2½ yards of lace for 1 combing cloth at £17	53	2	6
3⅛ yards of lace at £14	42	0	0
An apron of lace	17	0	0

The stern and gloomy William III does not at first appear as a man interested in lace, but he possessed in strong degree the Dutch taste for the fabric. In the year 1695–6, his lace bill amounted to £2,459 19s. Items charged included:

	£	s	d
To six point cravats	158	0	0
To eight point cravats for hunting	85	0	0
54 yards for 6 barbing cloths	270	0	0
63 yards for 6 combing cloths	283	10	0
117 yards of cut-work for trimming pocket handkerchiefs	485	14	3
78 yards for 24 cravats at £8 10s	663	0	0

The laced steinkirk was as fashionable in England as in France, and English military officers rivalled those of France in the richness of their lace ruffles and cravats.

INCREASING PROSPERITY OF ENGLISH LACE The lace industry of England continued to progress in the reign of William and Mary. Defoe wrote in 1724 of the industry at Blandford that it was flourishing and that lace was being sold at £30 per yard. He recorded also that 'through the whole southern part of Bedfordshire the people are taken up with the manufacture of bone lace in which they are wonderfully exercised and improved during the past years'. Devonshire and Buckinghamshire lace industries throve also, and the high quality and originality of English-made bobbin laces is proved by the export abroad. France had been for long a ready customer of English needlepoint lace. Its prestige in the French court was established at as early a date as 1638. In a letter written to the Duc de Luyens it was stated:

'To-day were brought to Madame de Luyens the laces she had chosen for the Queen, which, after use, reverted to the ladies of honour. They consist of coverlets trimmed with *point d'Angleterre* for the big bed, and of pillow-cases similarly trimmed. This set of things cost thirty thousand livres, Madame de Luyens not deeming it necessary to give orders as to the renewing of the best coverlets belonging to the Queen.'

Madame de Luyens was complimented on her economy in not spending a greater sum of money on these adornments as had been the practice with her predecessors.

Some authorities maintain that the demand for English lace far exceeded the supply and explain that ambiguous term *Point d'Angleterre* by the fact that much Belgian lace was sold under that name.

QUEEN ANNE Queen Anne wore lace profusely, though not to so extravagant a degree as her sister, Queen Mary. She did not patronize the native industries. At her coronation she favoured Flanders point. In one year she spent £1,000 in the purchase of her favourite varieties of bobbin lace, Brussels and Mechlin. Queen Anne endeavoured to boycott the laces of France which were being worn so extravagantly that they are reputed to have trimmed ladies' corsets. In 1711 she forbade the entry of gold and silver lace into England. Spanish point lace in gold and silver was favoured on state occasions to decorate dresses and mantles. Thread lace was used for the 'heads' and lappets of caps. The length of the lappets were indicative of the social rank of the wearer.

EXTRAVAGANCES OF FASHION Satirists poked fun at the extravagances of fashion and ridiculed those wearers of fine lace who possessed no shirts. Jabots were often enormous as were also the elaborate lace ruffles, 'weeping ruffles', worn at the wrist. Men of fashion wore these wrist ruffles falling over their hands. The cynical accredited their origin to a fashion among card-sharpers and throwers of dice who concealed their malpractices under the lace flounces. In later years, 'weeping ruffles' were said to be subterfuges for the passing of Jacobite missives and of clandestine notes.

Lace fashions had by now extended to retainers. The liveries of lacqueys were trimmed with jabots and ruffles. The servants of Queen Anne were subject to regular inspections. She required that their periwigs should be neatly dressed and their lace kept clean.

The Modern Warrior of 1756 shows that in this reign there was much thieving of lace and of the brooches set with precious jewels which were often used to fasten it.

A robbery at the house of a Lady Anderson in Red Lion Square, London, in 1700, included the loss of 'A head with fine loopt lace, of very great value; a Flanders lace hood; a pair of double ruffles and tuckers; two laced aprons, one point, the other Flanders lace; and a large black lace scarf embroidered in gold'.

The high *fontange*, or *commode*, rising tier upon tier continued in fashion for a time under Queen Anne. The women 'carried Bow steeple on their heads', said a writer, and such was the height of these fantastic head-dresses that the *Spectator* declared in 1711, 'the female of the species were much taller than the men who were as grasshoppers before them'.

Suddenly the fashion of the *commode* collapsed but it revived temporarily under George I.

LACE AN ARTICLE OF CURRENCY In his book, *The Lover*, Addison tells how, at the close of Anne's reign, lace became an article of currency. When the mania for collecting china first seized England, many a noble but impoverished lady exchanged her lace for punch bowls and mandarins. Many a duped husband bought his wife lace little knowing that she would exchange it for some china ornament.

By the end of the reign of Queen Anne, the lace-making industry of England had expanded in area. Centres were now established as far apart as Cambridge and Cornwall. Ladies of the upper classes, many of whom had been educated in France, employed their long leisure hours in making lace but this was for personal use and not for commercial purposes.

EARLY HANOVERIAN LACE With the establishment of the House of Hanover the lace mania expressed itself fully and extravagantly. At birth, at marriage, at death, at court, at the Old Bailey, at home, lace featured largely. Dean Swift, in his *Letters to a Young Lady*, said:

'And when you are among yourselves, how naturally, after the first compliments, do you entertain yourself with the price and choice of lace, and apply your hands to each other's lappets and ruffles, as if the whole business of your life and the public concern depended upon the cut of your petticoats.'

The scorn of a local dramatist writing at fashionable Tunbridge Wells in 1727 seethes through his words:

'Since your fantastical geers came in with your wires, ribbons and laces and your furbelows with three hundred yards in a gown and petticoat, there has not been a good housewife in the nation.'

At the royal and noble drawing-rooms the nobility appeared in 'borrowed lace'. The lace merchants interpreted the term 'borrowed' as unpaid and became all but bankrupt. Duns besieged the houses of these wearers of lace but the fashion prevailed.

ENGLISH LACES FOSTERED Fashions changed very little in the reign of George I, save that 'weeping ruffles' worn at the wrist grew yet more exaggerated in size. Brussels lace was still the favourite but the next reign saw deliberate efforts to foster native industries. There was a demand for English laces at the marriage of Frederick, Prince of Wales, in 1736. The Society of Anti-Gallicans was founded with a view to counteracting the taste for foreign laces and for fostering the lace industries of England. This society did much useful work in its quarterly meetings and awarded prizes for bone and point lace in addition to other crafts. At the same time, Acts of Parliament enforced the measures already taken to prevent the importation of gold and silver thread lace from foreign countries.

The lace mob cap tied with strings, and the lace apron which had been fashionable since the days of Queen Elizabeth grew *démodé* in the second half of the eighteenth century. Beau Nash, the Fashion King of the Regency period, is accredited with performing the funeral rites at Bath on the apron which he regarded as lacking that dignity so essential to high society. His biographer, Goldsmith, writing in 1752, stated:

'I have known him at a ball night strip the Duchess of Queensberry and throw her apron on one of the hinder benches among the ladies' women, observing that none save Abigails appeared in white aprons, though that apron was of the costliest point and cost two hundred guineas.'

LACE CHRISTENING ROBES Christening robes became vehicles for carrying immense quantities of rich lace, and the child was often wrapped in immense flounces of the fabric. The christening suit of a child included a robe, cap, mittens, shawl and pillow, all of which were elaborately trimmed with lace. The *Cornhill Magazine*, dated April 1864, in 'A Gossip on Royal Christening', tells of a pathetic incident following on the wearing of so much lace:

'George III and Queen Charlotte often condescended to become sponsors for the children of the aristocracy. To one child their presence was fatal. In 1778 they "stood" to the infant daughter of the last Duke and Duchess of Chandos. Cornwallis, Archbishop of Canterbury, officiated.

'The baby, overwhelmed by whole mountains of lace, lay in a dead faint.

'Her mother was so tender on the point of etiquette that she would not let the little incident trouble a ceremony at which a king and queen were about to endow her child with the names of Georgiana Charlotte. As Cornwallis gave the infant back to the nurse, he remarked that it was the quietest infant he had held.

'Poor victim of ceremony! It was not quite dead but dying; in a few unconscious hours, it calmly slept away.'

LACE-TRIMMED SHROUDS Lace-trimmed shrouds were used for burying the dead and the effigies of monarchs were decked with lace. This had long been the custom in England. When an Act of Parliament was passed stating that the dead were to be buried in *woollen* cloths a woman in London applied to William in 1678 for the monopoly of making *woollen laces* for the burial of the dead. Her boon was granted and the *London Gazette* of August 12th, 1678, carried this advertisement:

'Whereas decent and fashionable laces, shifts and dressings for the dead, made of woollen, have been presented to His Majesty by Amy Potter, widow, and His Majesty well liking the same hath, upon her humble petition, been graciously pleased to give her leave to insert this advertisement, that it may be known she now wholly applies herself in making both lace and plain of all sorts, at reasonable prices, and lives in Crane Court, in the Old Change, near St Paul's Churchyard.'

In after years many lace-makers followed Amy Potter in the pursuit of her lugubrious occupation.

Brussels lace was much favoured in the reign of George II, though it is fair to point out that native laces were also encouraged by this patriotic king. In the *Dictionary of Commerce*, 1766, Postlethwait raves indignantly against the vogue for Brussels lace:

' 'Tis but a few years since England expended upon foreign lace and linen not less than two millions yearly. As lace in particular is the manufacture of nuns, our British ladies may well endow monasteries as wear Flanders lace, for these popish nuns are maintained by Protestant contributions.'

PROTECTION FOR ENGLISH LACES UNDER GEORGE III In an effort to foster home industries George III gave orders that all the dress materials worn at the marriage of his sister Augusta to the Duke of Brunswick should be English made. The guests and attendants ignored this command and ordered laces freely from the Continent. Three days before the ceremony, the King ordered the custom officers to raid the workshops of the tailors, dressmakers and milliners and to confiscate all foreign goods.

George III waged constant war against the smuggling of lace and the newspapers of his reign are full of accounts of confiscations. Smuggling was practised by all sorts and conditions of men and women. A member of the Spanish Embassy was relieved by the custom-house officers of thirty-six dozen shirts, trimmed with elaborate Dresden ruffles and jabots and large quantities of lace meant for ladies' wear. The confiscated effects of a lord included: 16 black *à la mode* cloaks trimmed with lace; 44 French lace caps; 11 black-laced handkerchiefs; 6 lace hats; 6 ditto aprons; 10 pairs of ruffles; 6 pairs of ladies' blonde ditto, and 25 gentlemen's. The pocket of a footman was emptied of eleven yards of edging and six pairs of ruffles.

A lady of high rank was stopped in her sedan chair and deprived of a large amount of French lace. Some fashionable young ladies were stopped in the park; their black lace mittens were cut off their hands because they were of foreign manufacture. A poor old woman carrying a quartern loaf was arrested; the loaf contained £200's worth of lace. A Turk's turban was found to be stuffed with foreign lace valued at £90. Coffins were searched zealously for contraband, and with greater zeal when it became known that the High Sheriff of Westminster had been successful in bringing over, with the body of Bishop Atterbury of Rochester on its journey from Calais, lace to the value of £6,000.

ROYAL PATRONAGE George III deliberately encouraged the lace fabrics of England. Queen Charlotte favoured a fly cap with long lappets made of British lace. She had a magnificent lace dress made by the lace-workers of Lyme Regis. This dress caused much wonder at court, being made of the finest point. For their efforts the lace-workers received 4*d* a day as wages. Interest now centred in black and blonde laces. In 1775, Queen Charlotte established in London an institution for employing poor female children in the making of laces of this type.

Thread lace suffered disastrously in the nineteenth century when machine-made net was manufactured. Artistic merit was sacrificed for cheapness of fabric. In 1883 flax thread was replaced by cotton thread. This was not so effective a medium in the finished product although the lace-worker welcomed it as being less liable to break in the working. It was more elastic in texture and altogether easier to handle.

MANIA FOR COLLECTING OLD LACES A reaction against machine-made lace set in and there arose a mania among connoisseurs to possess the old hand-made laces of England and other countries. Some carried the reaction to the point of wearing all the laces they had acquired, and fashionable Englishwomen became the subject of ridicule. The Count of Syracuse is reported to have said: 'The English ladies buy a scrap of lace as a souvenir of every town they pass through, till they reach Naples, then sew it on their dresses, and make one grand toilette of the whole to honour our first ball at the Academie Nobile.'

INTEREST OF QUEEN ADELAIDE Deliberate efforts were made by Queen Adelaide, consort of William IV, to resuscitate the native lace industries of England. The distressed lace-workers of Devonshire had appealed to her for her patronage. Among other things, she ordered a dress to be made of Honiton lace bearing the traditional sprigs. She expressed a wish that the skirt should be encircled with flowers copied from nature. Her request was observed and the design was made up of flowers, the initials of each forming the name of the Queen – *A*maranth, *D*aphne, *E*glantine, *L*ilac, *A*uricula, *I*vy, *D*ahlia, *E*glantine.

QUEEN VICTORIA'S PATRONAGE Beer, a little fishing hamlet on the Devon coast, lying between Seaton and Exmouth, became one of the main centres of the revived industry. Here the wedding dress of Queen Victoria was made at a cost of £1,000. The Queen's interest in Honiton lace and the frequent visits of the court to Sidmouth helped to re-establish the vogue for Devon laces. The popularity of Honiton lace continued throughout the long Victorian era. The workers were supplied with new patterns and schools were established at various centres in the country. Public enterprise came to the support of private patronage and everything possible was done to perpetuate the old art. Interest continued to increase, however, in machine-made laces. They were so much cheaper and, in addition, a degeneracy of design set in rendering Devon work a decadent form of eighteenth-century *Point d'Angleterre* which some claim to have originated in this area.

EFFECT OF WORLD WAR I The fashion for laces waned in the twentieth century and the English hand-made laces received a mortal blow when, after the Great World War I, laces were made cheaply but artistically by Belgian and other refugees.

Lace Centres in Britain

The centres for making hand-made lace were scattered throughout the country in the sixteenth and seventeenth centuries, but at the close of the latter they tended to become more consolidated in the environs of Northamptonshire, Bedfordshire, Buckinghamshire and Devon. The repute of the better-known laces must not, however, blind one to the fact that there were other centres, which, if smaller, were very flourishing. There is romance in the thought that the lace-makers of the Isle of Man, the Isle of Wight and the Channel Islands, learnt their craft as an offshoot of the practice of smuggling lace through the islands. The flourishing lace centre at Ripon was a legacy from conventual days. In Wales, at Swansea, at Pontardawe, Llanwrtyd, and Brecon, a lace of the Valenciennes type was made and is believed to reflect the teachings of ladies interested in putting into practice the precepts of the Wesleyan faith.

The best of the English laces were considered cruder in design and coarser in texture than their Continental prototypes. Nevertheless, good work was done and the lace-workers of the Midland counties and of the south-west worked zealously at their traditional patterns, and at producing copies of the Continental laces, those of Valenciennes and Mechlin in particular.

English Needlepoint Lace

CONTROVERSY AS TO ORIGIN One of the most beautiful needlepoint laces of all times is that known as *Point d'Angleterre*. Overshadowed by the high reputation of the lace industries of the Continent, Britain never realized fully the worth of her own needlepoint lace. Controversy arose as to the real origin of *Point d'Angleterre*, for much Belgian work appeared under that name. Modern connoisseurs have succeeded not only in obtaining full recognition for the beautiful *Point d'Angleterre* as a British product but have succeeded also in exploding the myth that it was created by Belgian hands.

There appears to be no reason why Belgium, already long-established as a lace-making country of high repute, should invent a new type of lace and call it *Point d'Angleterre*. Nevertheless, there are those who hold that this variety of needlepoint *was* made in Brussels and call in evidence showing how needlepoint lace from that centre was smuggled into England when Charles II forbade, on economic grounds, the purchase of Brussels lace. The contraband lace was sold as having been made in Devonshire where lace of a similar design and execution was familiar. Those who support the view of Brussels manufacture also point out that Colbert, the minister of Louis XIV, determined to protect the infant lace industries of France, forbade the entry of Brussels lace into the country. The French court had, however, a decided preference for the laces of Belgium and vast quantities were smuggled into the country for their use under the name of English point. Colbert had not placed a ban on English laces. Some hold that he considered them too insignificant to compete against French fabrics. On the other hand, there is evidence that *Point d'Angleterre*, whatever its origin, was much esteemed in France.

EARLY NEEDLEPOINT   *Point d'Angleterre* existed long before the reign of Charles II. As far back as the reign of Queen Elizabeth there was shown an intense interest in needlepoint as a favourite pastime which England shared with France and other European countries. The close intercourse between England and France and the Netherlands in matters political and economic had social repercussions. In lace-work there was an interchange of ideas and models. In 1605 an Englishman, Mr Mignerak, published a book which contained a collection of well-known *Point Coupé* patterns and lace-bobbin patterns.

English needlepoint was imported in large quantities into France. Savory, in *Le Parfait Négociant*, in 1675, when Colbert's lace manufactories were flourishing in the country, wrote: 'There is a large importation from England of laces of silk and of linen thread.'

Such statements give ballast to the contention that in the second half of the seventeenth century the demand for English needlepoint lace exceeded the supply. There is intense satisfaction, therefore, in the pursuit of honest assessment in the reflection that much Belgian needlepoint was sold as *Point d'Angleterre* to meet the current need; this appears to be far nearer the truth than the claim that the reverse was the case.

Point d'Angleterre was one of the most exquisite of all needlepoint laces. According to the folk-lore of the lace industry, James Rodge of Honiton, who was to become famous as a seller of bone lace, escaped from Brussels, where he served as a valet, in the latter half of the sixteenth century and taught the lace-makers of the area the finer stitches practised in Flanders at the time.

CHARACTERISTICS OF 'POINT D'ANGLETERRE'   In *Point d'Angleterre* the *réseau* of exquisite softness was bobbin-made. Dainty workmanship characterized the pattern or *toile*. The threads of the ground were attached to the open edge of the *toile* and followed the curves of the pattern. In some specimens, high relief was introduced into flowers and leaves, not by the usual method of using a thicker thread but by plaiting and twisting the bobbins.

The *réseau* of English needlepoint was made in many varieties. The mesh varied considerably in size even within a single specimen. The brides, bobbin-made, enhanced the design. Where particular attention was given to the brides, the needlepoint was known as *Point d'Angleterre à brides*. The flowers usually had needlepoint fillings, finely executed.

English Bobbin Lace

Buckinghamshire Lace

The art of lace-making prospered for a greater period of time in Buckinghamshire than in the other Midland counties.

EARLY LACE SCHOOLS Much of the work was taught in lace schools. As elsewhere in Britain, the Buckinghamshire establishments were not elaborate. They were reasonably happy centres, filled with healthy, rosy-cheeked children; yet, in the light of more enlightened days some of the practices current in them appear as cruel barbarities.

The children had to work with great rapidity. They were compelled to sit for a considerable length of time without moving from the pillows. In many districts, the school-room itself was unwholesome and insanitary. The school itself was often just a small thatched cottage. Here children of seven and eight years of age, to the number of twenty or more, were housed for instruction in a low-ceilinged, ill-lit room. Each child carried to school a 'dickey-pot' – an earthenware jar filled with red-hot ashes. These served to heat the schoolroom, for no open fire was allowed in proximity to the white lace work. On the Continent it was the custom to build for the lace-workers a little room above the byre so that heat rising from the cattle and from the hay should penetrate into the fireless workroom.

The children, learning their craft in the lace school, worked for long hours at the elaborate and tedious technique. Yet, with the irrepressible spirits of youth, they found an outlet for suppressed energy in the singing of 'tells' as they worked.

One of the tells sung in Buckinghamshire ran:

> A lad down at Olney looked over the wall,
> And saw nineteen little girls playing at ball.
> Golden girls, golden girls, will you be mine?
> You shall neither wash dishes nor yet feed the swine;
> But sit on a cushion and sew a fine seam
> Eat white bread and butter and strawberries and cream.

'Golden girls' was the name given to the pins with gold-coloured heads which were stuck into the pillow to commence the lace. The nineteen little girls was a reference to nineteen pins which served as a special calculation mark in making the lace.

Lace had been made in Buckinghamshire before the Tudor period. Influxes of refugees had fostered the industry which soon began to flourish following on their interest. There was a severe set-back in the reign of James I on account of the granting of monopolies. The lace-workers of Great Marlowe sent a petition to the High Sheriff of the county describing their distress on account of the 'bone lace-making being much decayed'.

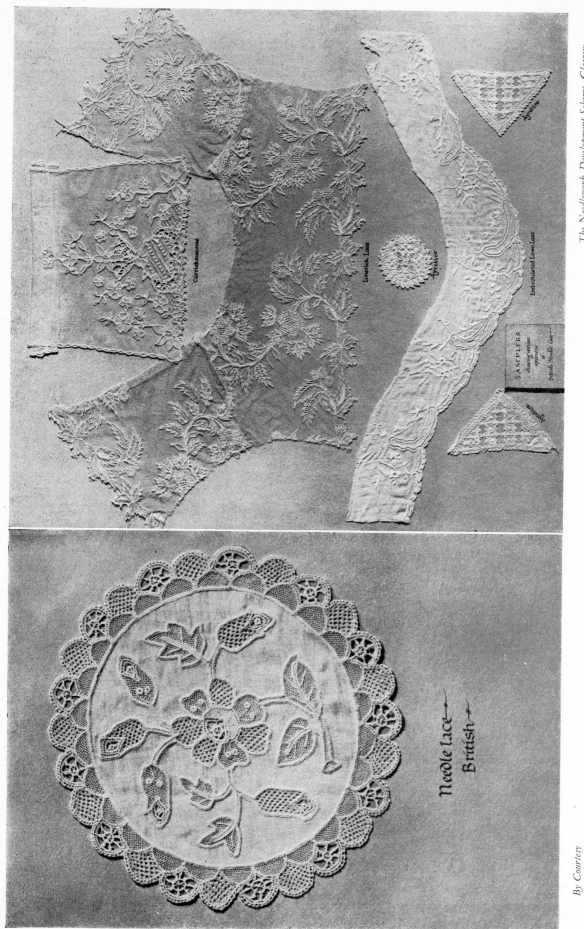

Needle Lace —
British —

Carrickmacross

Limerick Lace

Ayrshire

Embroidered Lawn Lace

Ayrshire

SAMPLERS
showing various
patterns
of
British Needle Laces

Ayrshire

By Courtesy   The Needlework Development Scheme, Glasgow

Great Britain. Needlelace. Mid-nineteenth century

Left: Mat. Flower design in white on fine lawn showing varied fillings and an attractive scalloped border
Right: Needlelace worked on net and lawn. Carrickmacross, Limerick and Ayrshire laces are included

LACE CENTRES IN BUCKS It is probable, therefore, that it was as a relief measure that Sir Henry Borlase founded and endowed a free school at Marlowe for twenty-four boys and for twenty-four girls. The girls were 'to knit, spin and make bone lace'. Lace was to become the staple product of the town and the fabric made here enjoyed a European reputation.

Other important centres of the lace industry were at Aylesbury, Newport Pagnell, Hanslape, Stoney Stratford and Olney.

The poet Cowper lived at Olney and the scene which he described in *The Winter Evening* must have been one which he had witnessed frequently, for the prosperity of the industry continued into the eighteenth century.

> Here the needle plies its busy task;
> The pattern grows, the well-depicted flower,
> Wrought patiently into the snowy lawn,
> Unfolds its bosom; buds and leaves and sprigs,
> And curling tendrils, gracefully dispos'd
> Follow the nimble fingers of the fair –
> A wreath that cannot fade, of flowers that blow
> With most success when all things else decay.

Cowper was to witness a temporary eclipse of the prosperity of Buckinghamshire lace. He wrote a petition to Lord Dartmouth saying that 'hundreds in this little village of Olney are on the point of starving and that the most unremitting industry is barely sufficient to keep them from it'.

But the industry prospered again and in 1752 the Anti-Gallican Society awarded the first prize for making the best piece of English pillow lace to one William Marriott of Newport Pagnell.

At the time of the French Revolution, the lace industry of Buckinghamshire benefited from the settlement of French refugees within its borders.

'BABY' LACE Much of the lace made in this area was of the narrow edging type which was much in demand for trimming baby clothes and dainty garments. Wide lace was also made. It resembled closely that made at Lille. The mesh of Buckinghamshire lace had a characteristic feature, being made of two threads twisted into a diamond shape. Sprays forming the design were worked on the pillow at the same time as the groundwork.

The designs of Old Bucks lace were limited but they were very attractive. The most widely adopted was that known as spider-lace. In this, the open mesh of the ground was introduced into the design. Brussels patterns and old Flemish work supplied the inspiration for many Bucks designs.

Bedfordshire Lace

The Flemings are reputed to have begun the lace industry of Bedfordshire and Buckinghamshire, following on their settlement in the neighbourhood resulting from the persecutions of the Duke of Alva. It is probable that Queen Catherine of Aragon only fostered and patronized a craft already established. French settlers came to the area after the Revocation of the Edict of Nantes and the industry continued to prosper. Defoe, writing of Bedfordshire in his *Tour Through the whole Island of Great Britain*, 1724–1727, recorded:

'Through the whole south part of this county, as far as the borders of Buckinghamshire and Hertfordshire, the people are taken up with the manufacture of bone lace, in which they are wonderfully exercised and improved within these few years past.'

As many as five lace schools were to be found in one village. Boys attended as well as girls.

WAGES OF LACE-WORKERS The wages of the lace-workers were comparatively low. In the mid-nineteenth century they seldom averaged one shilling a day; yet there is very little evidence of disaffection with wages. The standards of life were simple and the cost of living in that rural countryside was low. Cowper, the poet of the neighbouring county, could see in the lace industry an idyllic existence:

> Yon cottager who weaves at her own door,
> Pillow and bobbins all her little store;
> Content, though mean, and cheerful if not gay,
> Shuffling her threads about the livelong day;
> Just earns a scanty pittance, and at night
> Lies down secure, her heart and pocket light.

Bedfordshire lace resembled that of Lille. As in Bucks, much 'baby' lace was made. What was known as Regency Point was made for a period, and then the lace-workers advanced to the technique of plaited grounds. A feature was made in the county of straw-plaited laces. Straw known as Red Lanwas and White Chittein were obtainable from the midland and southern counties.

Northampton Lace

The bobbin laces of Northamptonshire were reproductions of Flemish laces. Old Flemish designs were copied well into the seventeenth century. Later, the lace-workers created fine grounds such as were characteristic of Brussels lace.

The year 1778 marked an advance, for it was then that the first 'point' ground was made. This term did not refer to needlepoint but to the rich effect of the *réseau*.

War with France in the closing years of the eighteenth century increased the lace trade of Northamptonshire. A *réseau* called locally 'French ground' was now made; it resembled that of the *fausse* type of Valenciennes.

Yak lace was also made in the county and in Buckinghamshire. This was a bobbin-made lace formed with wool obtained from the yak. Geometric and Maltese designs were copied in this medium. As in Buckinghamshire trolly lace was also made. 'Trolly' was a term used by the lace-workers with reference to the thick thread or *cordonnet*, introduced into the design.

Devonshire Lace

The laces of Devon enjoyed a wide reputation but the fame of the work must not be allowed to dominate completely that of lace fabrics made elsewhere in the south-west. Excellent laces were made in Wiltshire and in Dorset. Blandford, Sherborne and Lyme Regis were renowned for both needlepoint and bobbin laces.

Flemings settling in Devon after the Alva persecutions improved on the peasant laces already existing in the county. They urged the use of finer thread and introduced exquisite *jours* and fillings onto the designs.

JAMES RODGE   James Rodge is reputed to have been one of the prime promoters of the Devon lace industry at this period. A tombstone in Honiton Church testifies:

'Here lieth ye Body of James Rodge of Honiton in ye County of Devonshire, Bone-lace seller, who hath given unto the poor of Honiton Parish, the benyfite of 100L for ever, who deceased ye 27 July A. D. 1617. aetatis suae 50. Remember the Poore.'

Such was the reputation of Devon lace in 1660 that France issued a royal ordinance requiring that it should bear a special mark signifying its origin on being imported.

ECONOMIC MERIT OF DEVON LACE   Fuller, writing in his *Worthies of England*, praised the Devon lace industry. Referring to bone, or pillow lace, he said:

'Much of this is made in and about Honyton and weekly returned to London. . . . Modern is the use thereof and not exceeding the middle of the reign of Queen Elizabeth.

'Let it not be condemned for a superfluous wearing because it doth neither hide, nor heat, seeing it doth adorn. Besides, though private persons pay for it, it stands the State in nothing; not expensive of bullion like other lace, costing nothing save a little thread descanted on by art and industry.

'Hereby many children who would otherwise be burthensome to their parish, prove beneficial to their parents. Yea, many lame in their limbs and impotent in their arms, if able in their fingers, gain a livelihood thereby; not to say that it saveth some thousand of pounds yearly, formerly sent over Seas to fetch lace from Flanders.'

The Puritans showed an indulgence to the lace-making industry of Devon, for they were loath to injure its thriving commerce. At the time of Monmouth's Rebellion in 1680, the lace-workers suffered severely from the pillaging of the marauding soldiers. The industry revived and Defoe writing in 1724 recorded that the lace-manufacturing area extended from Exmouth to Torbay. Under Queen Victoria, the Devon lace industry flourished, but the Exhibition of 1851 with its display of attractive machine-made fabrics, caused a fatal injury to the hand lace-workers throughout the country.

The lace-makers of Devon in the seventeenth century made fabrics rivalling those of the Low Countries. The trolly lace also made in the south-west rivalled the Flemish varieties, although worked in a coarser thread. Devon 'Greek lace' was a simple torchon lace bearing a Greek or Maltese design. The lace-makers of Woodbury are said to have been trained in the making of this type when Queen Adelaide fostered the craft. Black lace, resembling Honiton, was also made in Devon.

Honiton was the main centre of the Devon lace trade. Boys as well as girls were trained in the lace schools, and lace-making became a subsidiary industry for men and boys waiting to go to sea or waiting for favourable conditions to work on the land.

HONITON LACE Honiton lace was famous for its sprays or sprigs. These were made with bobbins and applied to a net ground. The length of time required for making a hand-made ground and the quantity of fine Antwerp thread which went into its making resulted in the completed fabric becoming very expensive.

PAYMENT OF LACE-WORKERS Even in the mid-nineteenth century, the manner in which the Devon lace-worker was paid for her work was somewhat primitive. The lace fabric was spread upon the table. Shillings were laid upon it so as to cover it completely. As many coins as were required to cover the work was regarded as just payment to the lace-worker.

Devonia lace was a special kind of lace made in the last quarter of the nineteenth century. Relief was introduced into the inner areas of the design, giving a naturalistic representation of flowers, wings of butterflies, ferns and other motifs.

Here is a gift for your wedding morning,
A dainty kerchief of old, old lace.
It's many a year since I blushed behind it,
A bonny bride with a bright, young face.
Many a year since it lightly covered
A soft baby head with its angel gold;
As wife and mother my heart was happy
With all the sweetness that life could hold.

How will you look as a bride, I wonder,
For fashion changes each year, they say;
And now I am old and the world goes past me,
That world of wonders you see today.
And though you love me a little, darling,
Though you be fair for your bridal dressed,
Somehow I think 'tis an old world fancy
Old lace, old friends and old times are best.

LACE HEIRLOOMS Efforts have been made from time to time to resuscitate the lace industry of Devon which is not yet defunct. Pieces of old Devon lace are much prized and are sought out by collectors. Intrinsic value is great but there are treasured hand-made flounces fraught with yet greater sentimental value.

The lace-makers of Devon experienced a belated prosperity in the early twentieth century when they were called in to restore and re-make fine specimens of old lace. They gave a new lease of life to many torn and discarded fragments and showed considerable ingenuity in restoring old designs and grounds.

Suffolk Lace

Bobbin lace was made in Suffolk. It was a peasant variety employing the use of threads varying in thickness, causing a shadow effect. Laces were of the Torchon variety.

Much of the technique was traditional. Bones were cut into splinters to serve as pins and sheep's trotters were used as bobbins save when several hundred were required when they proved too combersome for use. Shakespeare was recording a picture familiar in the English country-side when he wrote in *Twelfth Night*:

> The spinsters and the knitters in the sun,
> And the free maids that weave their thread with bone.

The Laces of the Isles

ISLE OF MAN Many laces were sold under the name of Isle of Man lace. They were not of local manufacture. Until it was annexed to the British Crown, the Isle of Man was a prominent smuggling depot for French laces.

CHANNEL ISLANDS The Channel Islands were noted primarily for stockings and garments knitted in wool, but at the beginning of the nineteenth century an influx of French refugees led to a real interest in the manufacture of bobbin laces employing traditional French techniques and designs. Later, Jersey crochet work, as the lace was termed, experienced a vogue. The lace-workers imitated with surprising accuracy the old Venetian points.

ISLE OF WIGHT The interest of Queen Victoria in the lace industry of the Isle of Wight resulted in a revival of prosperity at a time when a rot of decline had set in. Needle-run lace was made after the manner of the Limerick laces. Designs were traced on waxed linen or parchment over which the net was tacked. The outlines of the design were run in double thread and a variety of filling stitches were used. Some of the work produced was exquisite and called for whole-hearted admiration.

English Lace in America

Many of the laces of the Midland counties of England and also those of Devonshire were carried across the Atlantic by eager and discriminating collectors. These laces helped to inspire in technique and design the lace-craft of America. The main demand was for cotton lace but silk laces were also desired. English traditions in craftsmanship and in design were adhered to closely and the workers favoured in particular round pillows such as those used by the Devon workers. Ipswich, Massachusetts, was a flourishing centre of the bobbin-lace industry.

The Lace of Scotland

The close bond uniting the Scottish and French courts led to a comparatively wide use of lace in the northern kingdom at an early date.

JAMES V   In the reign of James v, *passements* of gold and silver were in daily use. When Mary, Queen of Scots, returned to her native country from France, many varieties of lace became known. An inventory of the Queen's wardrobe in 1567 lists *passements*, *guimpeure d'or* and *guimpeure d'argent*.

Previous to the birth of her god-child, destined to be King James vi of Scotland and King James i of England, Queen Elizabeth is said to have sent to Mary a small basket lined with blue silk and trimmed with bone lace made of flax, rudely spun.

MARY, QUEEN OF SCOTS   Mary, Queen of Scots was herself an accomplished needle-woman. At the French court under the vigilant eye of her mother-in-law, Queen Catherine de Medici, she had been instructed in the arts of points and lacis according to the works of Vinculio. Of her talents as a needlewoman, there is ample proof in her will and in the relics of her workmanship preserved in those houses where she was held captive. She knitted head-dresses of 'gold reseille', with cuffs and collars of the same material. Her letters reveal constant requests for silk and other handicraft materials with which she might solace herself in her long captivity.

Mary made night-caps for Queen Elizabeth, which gifts were received with grace by that monarch although she recorded that 'great commotions had taken place in the Privy Council because she had accepted the gifts of the Queen of Scots. She therefore allowed them to remain for some time in the hands of La Mothe, the ambassador, but they were finally accepted'.

Mary's taste was definitely towards French laces. She obtained her lace ruffs from France. The Queen's every action was open to suspicion and an open and direct request for lace was inevitably associated with intrigue. This is evidenced in a letter written by Walsingham at Paris to Burleigh when the Queen was a prisoner at Sheffield.

'I have of late granted a passport to one that conveyeth a box of linen to the Queen of

Scots, who leaveth not this town for three or four days. I think that your Lordship shall see somewhat written on some of the linen contained in the same that shall be worth the reading.

'Her Majesty, under cover of seeing the fashion of the *ruffes*, may cause the several parcels of the linen to be held to the fire, whereby the writing may appear; for I judge there will be some such matter discovered, which was the cause why I did the more willingly grant the passport.'

The early portraits of Mary as Dauphine of France show her as wearing much gold *rezeuil* and *passement* on her dresses but she wore no thread lace. In a portrait taken at Lochleven Castle she wore a veil edged with narrow bone lace. At the time of her death on the scaffold she is said to have worn on her head 'a dressing of lawn edged with bone lace'.

JAMES VI AND AUSTERITY With the accession of James VI of Scotland who had been brought up as a strict Calvinist, a period of reaction against luxury in dress set in. By various enactments in 1581, 1597 and 1621, it was ordained that gold and silver lace could be worn only by noblemen, lords of sessions and prelates. No other members of the community had the right to wear pearlin on their 'sarkis and sokkis, their napkins and ruffles'. The word 'pearlin' was used for lace in the old Scottish language. Lace was the prerogative of the legal courts, and in the seventeenth century the lawyers of Scotland favoured close-fitting caps of velvet trimmed with lace.

Lace was regarded as 'devil's thread' by the Covenanters, and in 1672 they enacted the complete banishment of 'point lace made of thread'. Liveries were not to be trimmed with lace. A codicil of the enactment, however, allowed servants to wear out the old lace-trimmed clothes of their masters and mistresses.

The ban was observed rigidly and its effect was so disastrous on the lace-workers that, in 1674, the King made a concession and allowed the wearing of 'whyt lace by all and every person within this Kingdom'.

Poverty, the Covenanters and general legislation had, however, adverse effects on Scotland in general, and the demand for lace as well as for other luxuries waned. The Highlander decked out in full regalia still prided himself, however, on his falling band and ruffles made either of guipure or Flanders lace.

JACOBITE TASTE FOR LACE A fresh taste for fine laces was experienced when the Jacobites returned from the court at St Germain and introduced new French fashions into Scotland. During the period 1725–8, the Jacobite ladies are reputed to have worn voluminous gowns, measuring as much as nine yards in circumference. Their stone castles and houses had narrow winding staircases, necessitating to the minds of the ladies the use of under-clothing of a nature more luxurious than had ever been known before. Every lady of rank prided herself in the possession of a petticoat trimmed with the richest point lace which she exhibited at every opportunity by raising her hooped dress. She also wore a lace fly cap fitted with long lappets of fine lace.

In *Heart of Midlothian*, Sir Walter Scott gives a graphic description of a Scottish lady of 1745. She is Lady Lovat, the wife of Simon, the rebel:

'When at home, her dress was a red silk gown with ruffled cuffs and sleeves, puckered like a man's shirt, a fly cap of lace encircling her head, with a mob cap laid across it, falling down on the cheeks; her hair dressed and powdered; a lace handkerchief round the neck and bosom; a white apron edged with lace.'

SMUGGLING OF LACE Lace became an article of currency in the interest of the Jacobite cause, and many fine specimens were smuggled into Scotland from France. Some of the contraband lace was confiscated. The *Edinburgh Advertiser* of 1764 recorded how a parcel of rich lace had been taken secretly to the Duke of Devonshire. It reached him by accident having been intended for a nobleman, zealous in the Jacobite cause. On being opened out, the rich folds of lace revealed, hidden within, a miniature portrait of the Pretender set in a frame surrounded by large diamonds.

The smuggling of lace continued in the reign of George II. The officers of the Customs houses were either ignored completely or treated harshly, for the people regarded their presence as an unjust intrusion on their traditional rights.

THE PATRONAGE OF THE DUCHESS OF HAMILTON The Duchess of Hamilton – an irrepressible Irishwoman – was the main patroness of the lace industry of Scotland in the eighteenth century. French women whom she settled in Scotland taught local girls to make 'bunt lace'. Her enterprise was successful and the *Edinburgh Amusement* of 1754 recorded:

'The Duchess of Hamilton has now the pleasure to see the good effects of her charity. Her Grace's small orphan family have, by spinning, gained a sum of money and lately presented the Duke and Duchess with a double piece of Holland and some suits of exceeding fine ruffles of their own manufacture.'

It was mainly due to the efforts of the Duchess that there was founded in the year 1754 The Select Society of Edinburgh. Its purpose was to encourage the arts and manufactures of Scotland, and its work resembled that of the Anti-Gallican Society and the Dublin Society.

Lace-making was introduced into the schools and many an impoverished gentlewoman who had suffered in the Jacobite cause found in the making of fine needlepoint lace a means of subsistence.

No foreign laces were allowed in Scotland. English laces were, however, allowed to cross the border. There is no documentary evidence relating to the lace industry of Scotland after 1778. Hamilton lace, familiar through its lozenge pattern, continued to be made in scattered areas.

By Courtesy   *The Order of Poor Clares, Kenmare Convent*

Ireland. Irish Point. Late nineteenth century

Length: 14 inches   Width: 12½ inches

The figure represents Eire. She sits at her spinning wheel and
looks forward towards the round tower and bee-hive cells,
emblematic of her country and suggestive of its troubles

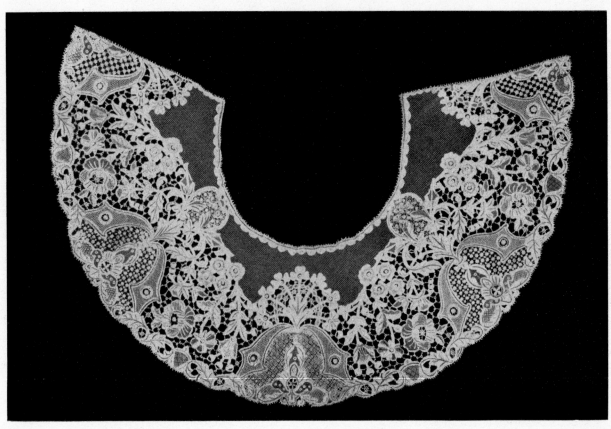

Ireland. Irish Point. Collar. Mid-nineteenth century
Motifs derived from Italian designs

The Lace of Ireland

The art of needlework was revered in Ireland even in the early Middle Ages. Giraldus Cambrensis, travelling in the island in the twelfth century, described a hooded mantle made of various pieces of cloth which were worked in squares with the needle.

English fashions were much favoured after the Rebellion. The Irish noblemen delighted in turn in the immense ruff with its handsome geometric designs, in the graceful falling band and in the rich cravat of Flanders lace.

FOSTERING OF NATIVE CRAFTS National sentiment resuscitated in Ireland in the eighteenth century. It expressed itself in a revived interest in the productions of the country. Notable among the promoters of this movement was Dean Swift. At a meeting held in 1722, he proposed the following resolution:

'That the ladies wear Irish manufactures. There is brought annually into this Kingdom near £90,000 worth of silk, whereof the greater part is manufactured; £30,000 more is expended in muslin, holland, cambric and calico. What the price of lace amounts to is not easy to be collected from the Customs-house book, being a kind of goods, that taking up little room is easily run; but considering the prodigious price of a woman's head-dress at ten, twelve, twenty pounds a yard, it must be very great.'

THE DUBLIN SOCIETY The patriotic Dublin Society which became incorporated in 1749 encouraged the making of pillow lace in Ireland. The Brussels variety of lace was favoured primarily. Thread used in the manufacture of Irish lace came from Hamburg. In 1765 the island imported 2,573 lbs.

An Act of the Irish Parliament of 1778 protected the Irish lace industry by prohibiting the entry of gold and silver lace from England and from all foreign countries.

RELIEF MEASURES In the nineteenth century the lace industry of Ireland was fostered as a relief measure following on national distress.

LIMERICK LACE Limerick lace-making was established as early as 1829. It was a form of tambour work made on Nottingham net. The industry represented the enterprise of Charles Walker, an Oxfordshire man who settled twenty-four girls as teachers of needle-run lace at Mount Kennet in Limerick. By 1855 the industry had flourished to the extent of employing 1,500 workers. By 1865, however, the number of workers had declined to 500. Large-scale emigrations to America were partly responsible for the depression in numbers.

VARIETIES OF IRISH LACE Further relief measures followed on the Great Famine of 1846. The lace industry of Ireland revived and was centred in many areas. Irish Brussels was made at Clones, Co. Monoghan; the finest Valenciennes at Lishnakea; Curragh Point was made at Curragh, Co. Limerick. Point lace was also made at Youghal and Irish guipure lace at Carrickmacross. Crochet lace-making was another Irish speciality and many girls taught in the Irish convents learnt to do exquisite crochet-work. In this no parchment or paper was needed, and it is fortunate that the workers took some of the finest of old laces as their models.

The guipure laces of Ireland were of two kinds. The *appliqué* was made on machine-made net. The pure guipure was made on the finest Mull muslin or lawn on which a design had been traced. The outline of the design was emphasized either with a thread or by a line of fine overcasting. The centres of the flowers were cut away and open-work stitches were made as fillings. Bars ornamented with picots or pearls united the various separate pieces of the design. When the pattern was complete, the muslin was cut away close to the outline of the design.

Conclusion

Lace has a universal appeal. Like every other form of craft, it experiences periods of marked prosperity and then sinks into near-oblivion for a time; but the demand for hand-made laces and their machine-made prototypes is never wholly obliterated.

CHARACTERISTICS OF OLD SPECIMENS   Fragile lace-work of many varieties leaves the observer awed with admiration. The durability of many of the old specimens is such as to leave one spellbound for the gossamer fabric has in many instances long outlasted the cloth for which it was intended. The eye revels among the wealth of designs created by our unlettered ancestors. Examining the exquisite honeycomb and point lace, the rose and leaf motifs, the gossamer webs of spider work, one is once more face to face with the eternal truth that modernity has not all the facets of advance on its side.

Lace fabrics are, of necessity, weighted with all the romace of the past for they have been a form of decoration beloved by king and by peasant. The courts of kings, the churches of many lands, the soldiers of opposing armies, men and women at home and abroad have all delighted in the possession of laces, and an aureole of personal interest surrounds each specimen which has been preserved.

Interest in the revival of old hand-made laces is marked and has been sponsored by several women's organizations. This is natural, for lace-making is an artistic outlet of real worth.

Dress designers and interior decorators are creating fresh demands for lace fabrics. Many people, in no way connected with the lace industry, are showing a keen interest in the evolution and practice of the craft.

MODERN INTERPRETATION   Lace centres of modern days tend to foster the creation of needle-run laces but they turn to the past for inspiration in their designs. Keen enthusiasm is being coupled to practical interest in the revival of the industry. Schools of lace and of stitchery have done valuable research work, collecting data relating to laces of the past and they have circulated old specimens for reproduction and for guidance. The result is that much modern work is beautiful and shows a virility which is individual. Lace-workers and lovers of lace are finding that it is well worth while to delve into the history and tradition of old lace-craft. There is truth in the dictum of an old Swedish lace-worker. 'Lace-craft slumbers; it does not die.'

Bibliography

BROOKE *Lace in the Making*

COLE *Ancient Needlepoint and Pillow Lace*

COLE *Of Lace*

JACKSON *The History of Handmade Lace*

KELLOGG *Bobbins of Belgium*

LEFEBURE *Dentelles and Guipures*

LEFEBURE *Les Points de France*

MOORE *The Lace Book*

POLLEN *Seven Centuries of Lace*

WHITING *A Lace Guide for Makers and Collectors*